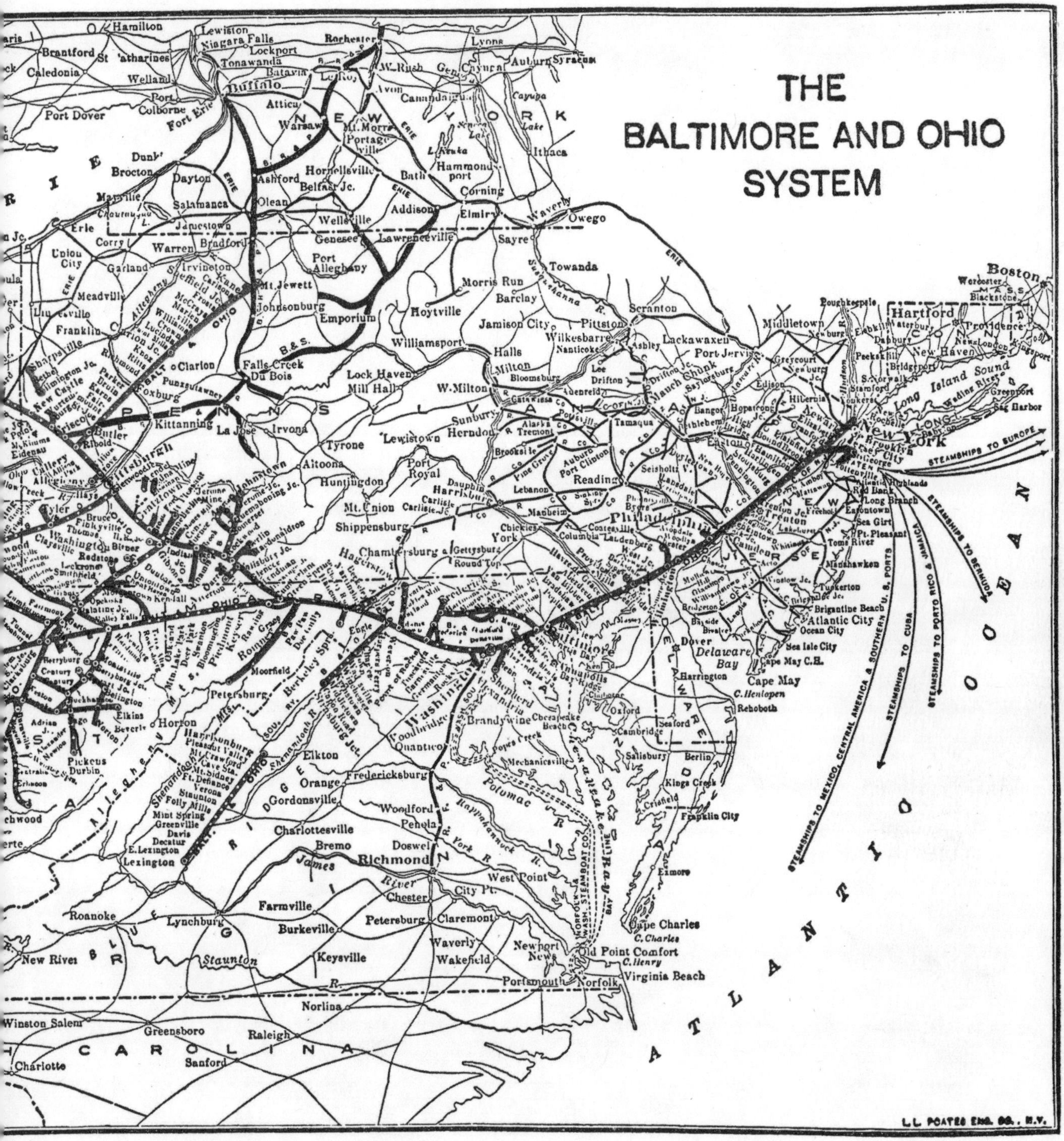
THE BALTIMORE AND OHIO SYSTEM
Hamilton
Lewiston
Niagara Falls
Rochester
Lyons
Brantford
Lockport
Tonawanda
Auburn
Syracuse
Caledonia
Welland
Batavia
Buffalo
Port Dover
Colborne
Fort Erie
Attica
Warsaw
Ithaca
Brocton
Dayton
Hornellsville
Bath
Hammond port
Ashford
Belfast Jc.
Corning
Salamanca
Olean
Addison
Elmira
Waverly
Owego
Wellsville
Erie
Jamestown
Genesee
Lawrenceville
Sayre
Corry
Warren
Bradford
Union City
Garland
Port Allegany
Towanda
Mt. Jewett
Meadville
Kane
Morris Run
Barclay
Boston
Johnsonburg
Franklin
Emporium
Hoytville
Jamison City
Pittston
Scranton
Middletown
Hartford
Providence
Williamsport
Wilkesbarre
Lackawaxen
Clarion
Falls Creek
Du Bois
Lock Haven
Mill Hall
Halls
Milton
Port Jervis
New Haven
Butler
Kittanning
La Jose
Irvona
W. Milton
Sunbury
Herndon
Mauch Chunk
Long Island Sound
Greenport
Sag Harbor
Tyrone
Lewistown
New York
Pittsburgh
Altoona
Huntingdon
Port Royal
Harrisburg
Reading
STEAMSHIPS TO EUROPE
Johnstown
Mt. Union
Carlisle
Lebanon
Shippensburg
Chambersburg
Gettysburg
York
Columbia
Philadelphia
Trenton
Long Branch
Sea Girt
Hagerstown
Frederick
Baltimore
Camden
Toms River
Washington
Wilmington
Tuckerton
Atlantic City
Ocean City
Brigantine Beach
Sea Isle City
Cape May C.H.
Cape May
Dover
Delaware Bay
Harrington
Moorfield
Petersburg
Berkeley Spgs.
Horton
Harrisonburg
Elkins
Cape Henlopen
Rehoboth
Seaford
Cambridge
Salisbury
Berlin
Brandywine
Quantico
Elkton
Orange
Fredericksburg
Gordonsville
Kings Creek
Crisfield
Franklin City
Pickens
Durbin
Woodford
Charlottesville
Bremo
Doswell
Richmond
Lexington
James River
West Point
Eimore
Farmville
City Pt.
Chester
Roanoke
Lynchburg
Burkeville
Petersburg
Claremont
Cape Charles
C. Charles
Waverly
Newport News
Old Point Comfort
C. Henry
Virginia Beach
New River
Keysville
Wakefield
Staunton
Portsmouth
Norfolk
Norlina
Winston Salem
Greensboro
Raleigh
CAROLINA
Charlotte
Sanford
STEAMSHIPS TO MEXICO, CENTRAL AMERICA & SOUTHERN U. S. PORTS
STEAMSHIPS TO CUBA
STEAMSHIPS TO PORTO RICO & JAMAICA
STEAMSHIPS TO BERMUDA
ATLANTIC OCEAN
L. L. POATES ENG. CO., N.Y.

BALTIMORE & OHIO STEAM LOCOMOTIVES

THE LAST 30 YEARS: 1928-1958

by

Peter Jehrio

and

Terry Sprague

TLC

PUBLISHING INC.

1387 Winding Creek Lane
Lynchburg, Virginia 24503-3776

Dedicated to:
Jean Jehrio
(by Peter Jehrio)

and

The friendly employees of the Baltimore & Ohio
(by Terry Sprague)

International Standard Book Number 1-883089-90-5
Library of Congress Control Number: 2003104160

Design and Layout by
Peter Jehrio
North Tonawanda, New York 14120

Printing by
Walsworth Publishing Company
Marceline, Missouri 64658

Produced on the MacOS™

First Printing 2003

ON THE FRONT COVER:

(above) Mountain #5584 rolls through Mance, Pennsylvania, in March, 1955, with her train in tow.
(William P. Price photo, Harry Stegmaier collection)

(below) Mountain #5565 opens up on a straight stretch, in 1955.
(Harry Stegmaier collection)

ON THE BACK COVER:

(above) A Pacific glides through Philippi, West Virginia, with train #135, on June 9, 1955.
(William P. Price photo, Harry Stegmaier collection)

(below) EM-1 #7600 overwhelms the turntable at Cumberland, Maryland, in September, 1956.
(Harry Stegmaier collection)

ACKNOWLEDGMENTS

We would like to thank Thomas W. Dixon, Jr., for his kind support throughout this project. He provided the photographs we used, the original concept for the book, and a draft of the introduction.

Next, this book would not have been possible without contributions from many photographers and collectors, including: the B&O Railroad; Howard N. Barr; Tom Batesman; Charles B. Chaney; Thomas W. Dixon, Jr.; G. A. Doeright, Jr.; Paul Dunn; Bruce D. Fales; R. J. Foster; Ted Gay; Robert Graham; R. C. Grey; Ed P. Haines; W. R. Hicks; Robert Hundman; William Kuba; Joseph Lavelle; William P. Price; Railroad Avenue Enterprises; John A. Rehor; Leonard W. Rice; Karl E. Schlachter; Joseph Schmitz; Donald A. Somerville; Harry Stegmaier; Bruce Triplett; R. Van Boven; Harold K. Vollrath; and Jay Williams.

Finally, we appreciate the assistance of Katey Ramsey, in both image preparation and book design.

ABOUT THE AUTHORS

Peter Jehrio has written or edited eight books about railroading, history, and travel, as well as many articles, commentaries, and short stories. Having grown up along both the Erie and New York Central Railroads, he has photographed trains for many years, and recently completed a 25,000-mile trip by train for a forthcoming book.

Terry Sprague grew up along the Baltimore & Ohio, has both observed and ridden on its steam engines, and was always impressed with the "mainline performance" of his branch-line's operation. He has restored various railroad equipment and structures.

TABLE OF CONTENTS

(above) Q-4 #4606, a Mikado, works a freight at Halethorpe, Maryland, on June 25, 1939.

(Leonard W. Rice photo)

Baltimore & Ohio (B&O) railroaders were a very special breed and, with over a hundred years of tradition and service behind them, deliverered their goods and passengers on time.
(Leonard W. Rice collection)

INTRODUCTION

We have done this book to present a remarkable collection of photos of B&O steam locomotives taken in the last, greatest, and best remembered era of their use. Included are both action and portrait photos of the most important classes of engines in service from the time of the Great Depression, through World War II, and down to the end of steam on May 17, 1958.

Our hope is these photos will be useful to modelers, and to the many fans and historians who study the B&O, making it one of the most popular railroads in American history.

This book does not attempt to be comprehensive in the treatment of any B&O class, nor to present detailed technical data. It is intended as an album of steam photos.

Several books have been published on the B&O in recent years which are recommended. First and foremost is Lawrence Sagle and Alvin Staufer's classic work, *B&O Power*, printed in 1964. Also essential in any collection on the line are several fine works by Charles Roberts, including *Sand Patch* and *East End.* For those who prefer color, there are two very good titles from Morning Sun Books. Finally, the B&O Historical Society publishes solid material on the line and its history, in their highly recommend bi-monthly magazine.

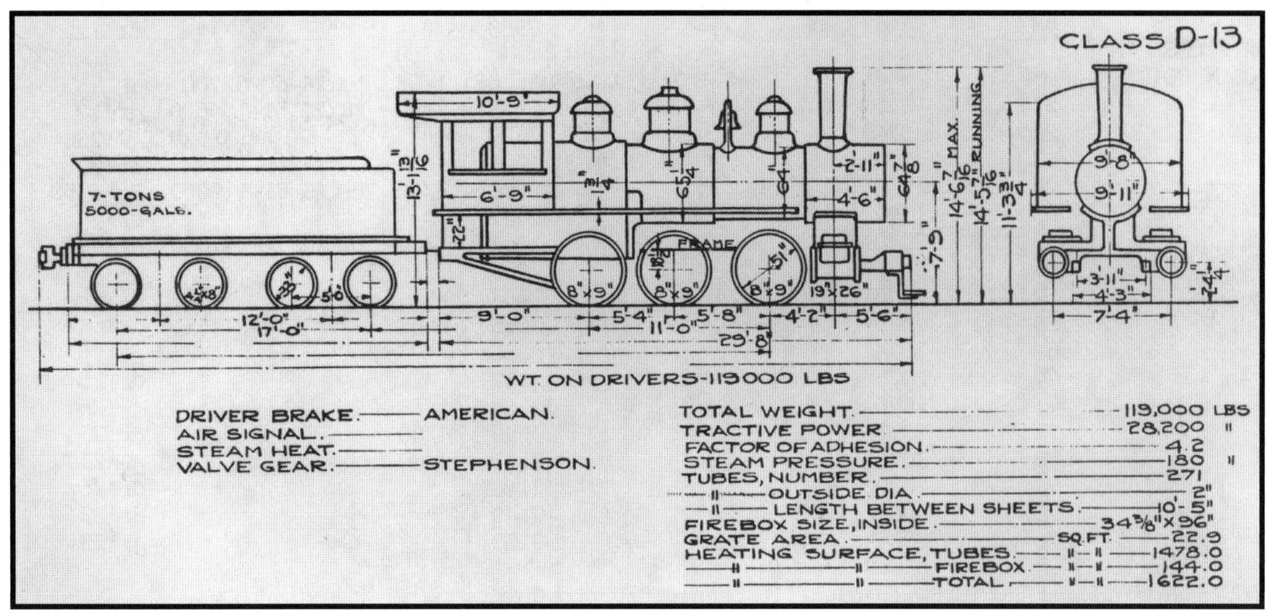

(below) A rather clean looking D-7, #1135, rests at Washington, in 1940. The photographer caught the switcher, with 50-inch drivers, in a classic "rods-down" pose. Note the extra headlight above the pilot.

(Bruce D. Fales photo)

(above) Tank engine #316, ex-#243, features the horse-friendly, "house on wheels" look in this 1909 view. Built in 1865, she was re-built two more times in her tenure with the road. The glass-wall enclosure was supposed to hide the more frightening aspects of the steamer from horses (one of which looks on a bit disinterestedly from afar). This New York City scene also offers a glimpse of a Lehigh Valley Railroad facility.

(Joseph Lavelle photo)

(above right) D-3 #42 is seen at Baltimore, on May 4, 1913.

(Karl E. Schlachter photo)

(center right) D-3 #1114, built by Baldwin, in 1892, idles at Brunswick, Maryland, in this 1945 view. Notice the several differences between this engine and the one immediately above it: the electric vs. oil headlight, the air tank under the cab, the position of the air pump, the cab windows, a full vs. slope-back tender, and the lettering on the tender.

(Bruce D. Fales photo)

(below right) D-22 #1120, seen in Cincinnati, Ohio, on September 5, 1952, was built by the Rhode Island Locomotive Works in 1890. Looking almost like a Spartan design from southeastern Europe, the (partial) tank engine is a shop switcher with an all-enclosed cab (designed perhaps with safety in mind). The coal bunker is inside the cab of this ex-Baltimore & Ohio Southwestern (B&O SW) locomotive.

(R. C. Grey photo)

B & O

1114
BALTIMORE AND OHIO

1120

94
BALTIMORE AND OHIO

1181
1181
BALTIMORE AND OHIO

80
BALTIMORE AND OHIO

(above) D-7 #1144 is shown here in Washington, District of Columbia, on September 25, 1940. The 40 engines in this class were built by both the Richmond Locomotive Works and Baldwin, in 1901 and 1903.

(Leonard W. Rice photo)

(above left) D-29 #94, seen at Cincinnati, in July, 1919, features an oil headlight. The ex-Cincinnati, Hamilton & Dayton (CH&D) #54 was built by the Pittsburgh Locomotive Works in 1900-1901.

(Karl E. Schlachter photo)

(center left) D-23 #1181 looks in sad shape, viewed at Mount Clare Yard, in Baltimore, on July 22, 1946. She may be awiting shopping, however. The camelback was built by Baldwin in 1906.

(Howard Barr photo)

(below left) D-40a #80 is seen in Buffalo, New York, on April 6, 1939. Featuring a new electric headlight, the switcher had a somewhat interesting heritage. Built by Baldwin in 1925, she is ex-Chicago & Alton (C&A) B-3 #80, and was renumbered #345 in 1944, by the B&O.

(Leonard W. Rice collection)

3 EIGHT-WHEEL SWITCHERS

(above) L-1 #1028 drills cars in the yards at Akron Junction, Ohio, on a cold and blustery day in January, 1946. The engine was re-built from 2-8-0 #2284.

(Bruce Triplett photo, Jay Williams collection)

Over the years, the ever-frugal B&O used rails made surplus from their continuing main-line upgrade work to do likewise in the major yard facilities.

The added weight of this newer rail allowed for the use of the 0-8-0, a heavy-weight switcher, in the same places.

The 0-8-0s were also a product of the road's frugality—a large number of them were rebuilt from early 2-8-0s.

Even with eight driving wheels, they were still able to navigate the typical yard curves, and easy for crews to handle. Most important, their increased power allowed these engines to become the main switcher for the line.

Also, with their added power, they became *the* engine to use in the heavy-tonnage facilities in places like New Castle, Pennsylvania, and Lorain, Ohio (while still being assigned throughout the B&O system).

In these places, they drilled with *heavy* strings of loaded hoppers, moving coal from the mines to the giant Great Lakes boats that would carry the commodity to the waiting steel mills. This added utility ensured that these engines would last to the very end of steam.

The 0-8-0s were assigned the L class, and numbered in the 600s, 700s, and 1000s. After 1956, they were re-numbered in the 1600s.

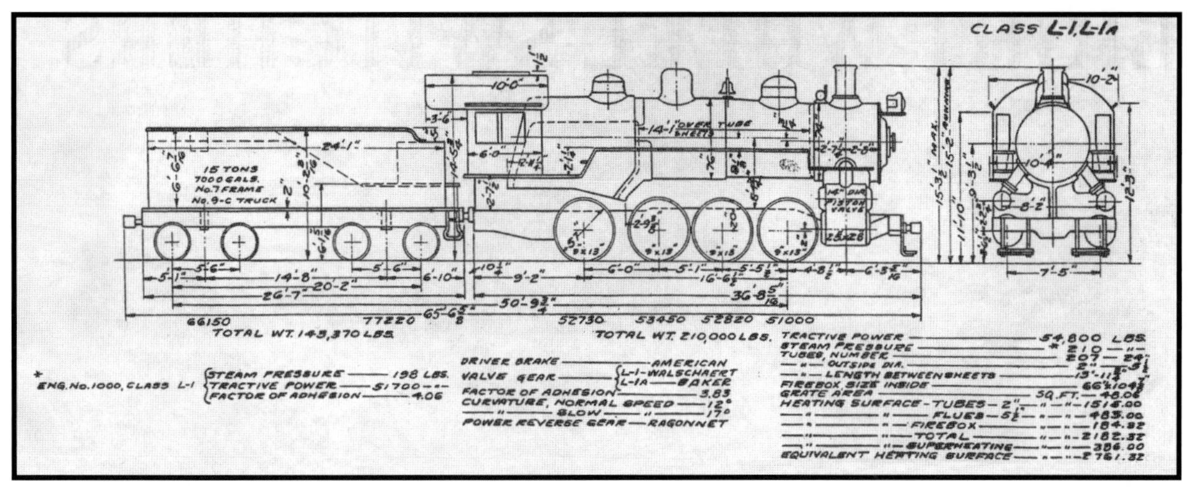

(below) L-2 #1633 sits in the service tracks at Grafton, West Virginia, on October 25, 1955. After the 1956 renumbering, she was #847.

(Leonard W. Rice photo)

(above) L-1 #1041 poses (with rods down, and the engineer looking passively from the cab window) in Washington, in 1940. She was re-built from 2-8-0 #2358, in 1925.

(Bruce D. Fales photo)

(above right) L-1a #1050 simmers away in New Castle, on June 28, 1939. She was formerly 2-8-0 #2208.

(G. A. Doeright photo)

(center right) Another L-1a, #1055, is seen in Washington, toward the end of the 1930s. She was converted from 2-8-0 #2305 in 1925.

(Leonard W. Rice photo)

(below right) Switcher #1043, like her 200-some sisters, was re-built from a 2-8-0 by the ever cost-conscious B&O. She was formerly #2380.

(Bruce D. Fales photo)

1050
1050
BALTIMORE AND OHIO

1055
BALTIMORE AND OHIO

1043
BALTIMORE AND OHIO

843
BALTIMORE AND OHIO
843

601
601
BALTIMORE AND OHIO

849
849
BALTIMORE AND OHIO
849

(above) L-2b #1606, seen in Painesville, Ohio, in July, 1955, would become #826 within a year, and have her fire dumped forever shortly after that. She is seen resting here between her duties.
(William Kuba photo, Jay Williams collection)

(above left) The end is at hand. It is August 25, 1958, and steam has been officially gone now for three months on the B&O, with the exception of a few switchers running in the Cleveland, Ohio area. Not so for *this* switcher, #843 (formerly #1628), which sits in the deadline in Benwood, West Virginia, awaiting a now all-but-certain fate. Any guesses?
(Thomas W. Dixon, Jr. collection)

(center left) L-2 #601 looks almost new in this company photo, taken in 1927, not long after her conversion from 2-8-0 #2515. Built in 1905, she was re-built in 1925.
(B&O photo)

(below left) Switcher #849 had been #1635 prior to the major renumbering effort in 1956. The changes were necessitated by all the diesels which had come onto the roster. She is seen in Cleveland, in 1957.
(Thomas W. Dixon, Jr. collection)

(above) L-2b #683 had been 2-8-0 #2616, up until 1928. Here, a decade later, she is seen in Clarksburg, West Virginia, on July 27, 1939.

(Howard Barr photo)

(above right) L-2c #711 takes a break in Baltimore's Riverside Yard, in 1935. She was re-built from 2-8-0 #2638.

(Leonard W. Rice photo)

(center right) Switcher #699 is found in Chicago, Illinois, at one of the western ends of the system, on September 29, 1951.

(Thomas W. Dixon, Jr. collection)

(below right) L-2 #601 sits beside the huge coaling station in Cumberland, Maryland. Built in 1905, as a 2-8-0, she was formerly #2515.

(Bruce D. Fales photo)

711
711
BALTIMORE AND OHIO

699
699
BALTIMORE AND OHIO

601
601
BALTIMORE AND OHIO

526

779
BALTIMORE AND OHIO

1056
BALTIMORE AND OHIO

(above) Switcher #1616, which became #833 after 1956, steams on the ready track at an unknown location.

(Leonard W. Rice collection)

(above left) Ex-Buffalo, Rochester & Pittsburgh (BR&P) #526, still in the lettering of its former owner, sits in Buffalo, New York, on July 20, 1933, not long after the January 1, 1932 takeover of the line by the B&O. Built by the Brooks Locomotive Works, she would become #778. Note the modified slope-back tender with the high coal bunker.

(Robert Graham photo, Jay Williams collection)

(center left) Here is another ex-BR&P engine, only this time in B&O lettering. An L-4, as is the locomotive above, #779 was built by Brooks, and would be retired in 1955. With her former owner, she was #527.

(B&O photo)

(below left) L-1a #1056 had been owned by the B&O all her life, however, she started out as 2-8-0 #2399. Seen here in Washington, on September 5, 1940, she was converted in 1926.

(Leonard W. Rice photo)

(above) U #951 sits proudly, rods down, in New Castle, on May 27, 1934. Built by Baldwin in 1914, she was originally a *slow* 2-10-2, #6030, before being converted into a still slow, but more usefully slow switcher.

(B&O photo)

4 TEN-WHEEL SWITCHERS

With the really *huge* 0-10-0s, the ever-resourceful B&O solved, at least partially, the problem of what to do with some of the earlier 2-10-2s, which proved simply too slow for mainline service--even with *slow* drags. The railroad once again turned to its remarkable crew of people at the Mount Clare Shops, and converted the crawling, but very powerful beasts into 0-10-0 switchers.

Taking advantage of the Santa Fe type's large boilers, low drivers, and heavy tractive effort, the line used the new switchers in hump yard and other heavy-duty switching chores.

The engines—only two of them were ever assembled—were assigned to the U class, and numbered in the 900s.

Despite their strength, however, the two powerful brutes were taken out of service in the early 1950s.

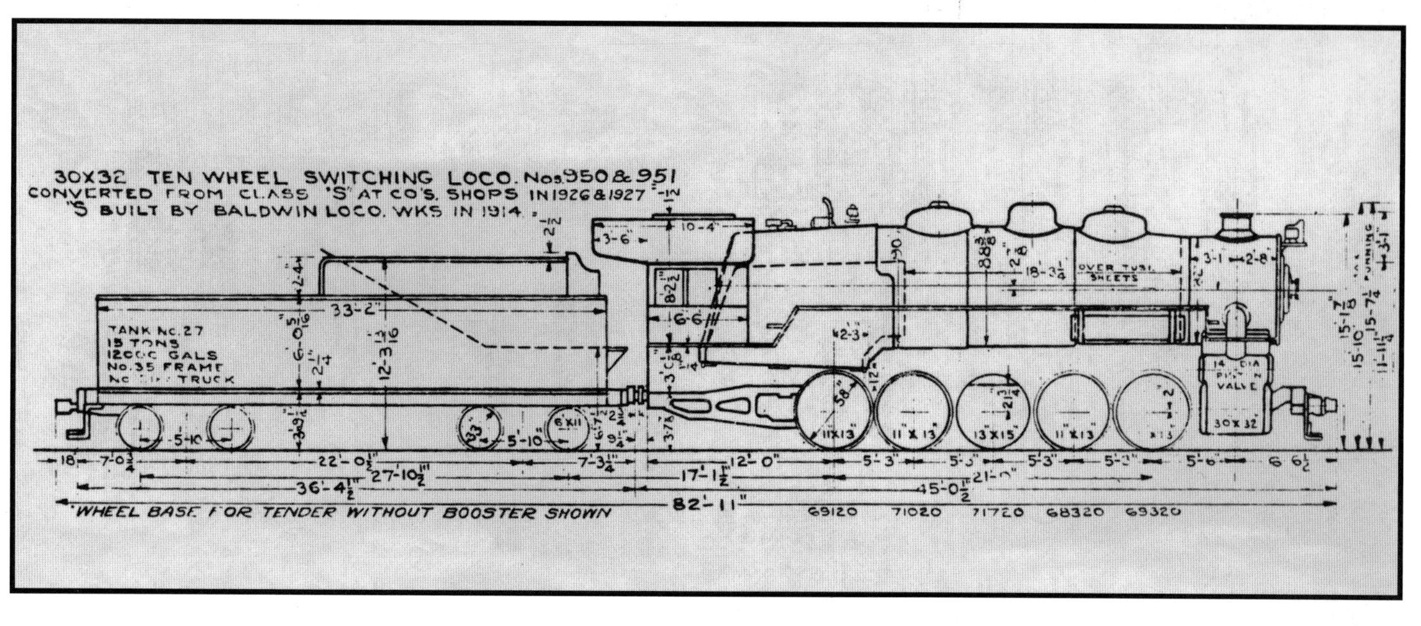

(below) In this early view, we see U #950, with rods down and lots of detail visible. She was re-built in the Mount Clare Shops, from S #6009, in 1926.

(Leonard W. Rice collection)

(above) K-20 #2430 was one of the heavier 2-6-0s stabled on the B&O, and is seen at Akron Junction, Ohio, on August 3, 1947,

(Harold K. Vollrath photo, Jay Williams collection)

5 MOGULS

The 2-6-0s did not last long in the modern era on the B & O, what with the early emergence of the much more powerful 2-8-0, and then the awesome proliferation of that newer type.

The twenty Moguls on the modern roster were assigned the K class, and numbered in the 900s and 2400s. The former group of engines, built by Baldwin in 1911, were all taken out of service by 1949. The latter group, built by Lima, lasted until 1954—but still left service almost four years before steam power eventually met its demise on the railroad.

One reason why the 2400s outlasted the 900s was that the 2400s were much bigger than the others, comparatively speaking.

Both classes of the small engines were used for light freight service, especially on branch lines. However, since this type of service was being phased out after the 1940s, there was no future for the Moguls.

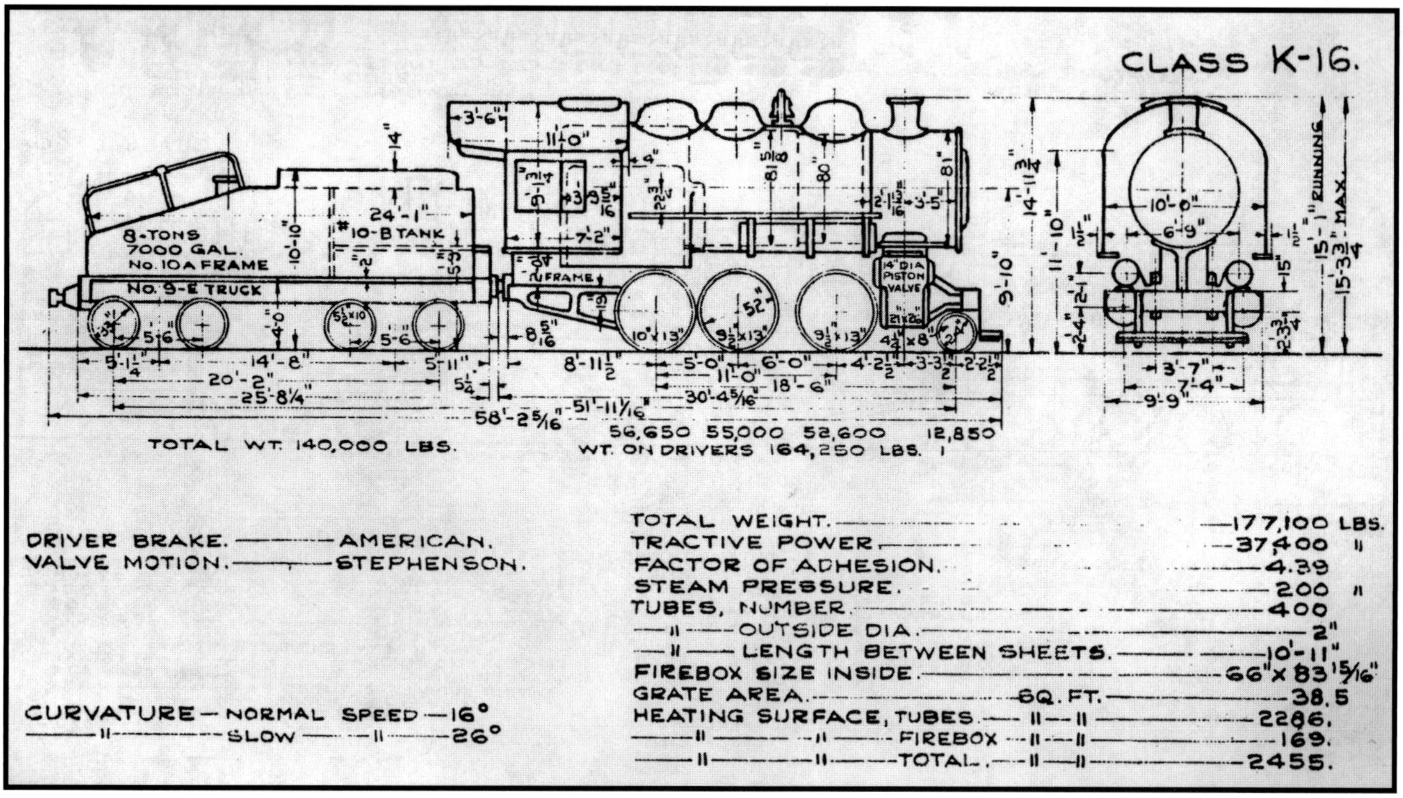

CLASS K-16.

8-TONS
7000 GAL.
No. 10A FRAME
#10-B TANK
No. 9-E TRUCK

TOTAL WT. 140,000 LBS.

56,650 55,000 52,600 12,850
WT. ON DRIVERS 164,250 LBS.

DRIVER BRAKE.——AMERICAN.
VALVE MOTION.——STEPHENSON.

CURVATURE — NORMAL SPEED — 16°
—— " —— SLOW —— " —— 26°

TOTAL WEIGHT.	177,100 LBS.
TRACTIVE POWER	37,400 "
FACTOR OF ADHESION.	4.39
STEAM PRESSURE.	200 "
TUBES, NUMBER.	400
— " — OUTSIDE DIA.	2"
— " — LENGTH BETWEEN SHEETS.	10'-11"
FIREBOX SIZE INSIDE.	66" x 83 15/16"
GRATE AREA. SQ. FT.	38.5
HEATING SURFACE, TUBES. — " — "	2286.
— " — " — FIREBOX — " — "	169.
— " — " — TOTAL. — " — "	2455.

(below) Here we see another Mogul of the same K-20 class, #2431. This one, built by Baldwin in 1911, is seen in Baltimore's Riverside Yard, on March 31, 1940.

(Leonard W. Rice photo)

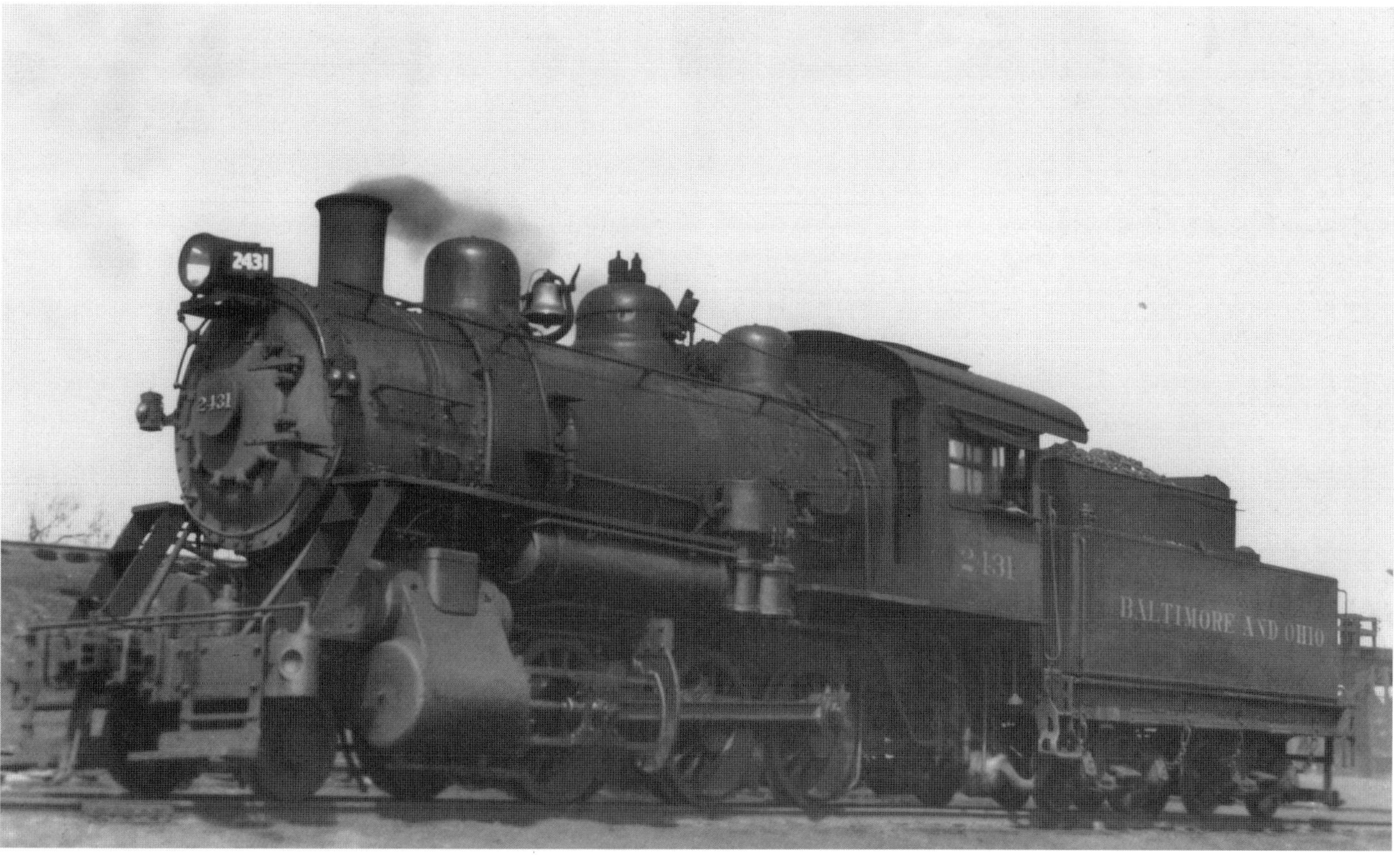

(above) E-27ca #207, one of so many 2-8-0s on the line, trundles across a trestle in a small city somewhere on the line, just before the end of steam. Her fire is burning clean, as witnessed by the clear stack. Before the 1956 renumbering, she was #2784.

(John A. Rehor photo)

6 CONSOLIDATIONS

The 2-8-0s were by far the most numerous type of engine on the B&O, with more than 800 of the engines on the modern roster alone!

All were assigned the E class (with over two dozen sub-classes), and were numbered in the 300-500s, 1200s, 1500-1900s, 2200-2300s, and 2500-3100s.

Until the Mikados came along, the 2-8-0s were *the* freight engine on the railroad (although, unlike the 2-8-2s, they were not often used in passenger service).

As witnessed by the large number of sub-classes, the 2-8-0s were the basis for many motive power experiments. A number of them even featured the "Pennsy" look, with Belpaire fireboxes, and the distinctive cabs of the B&O's rival.

Even without this experimentation, the type had an interesting history on the line, with major functional varieties (e.g., camelbacks), functional changes (e.g., conversions to and then back again from camelback, as well as between compound and simple use of steam), and the addition of so many varieties from the smaller lines the B&O acquired over the years.

There were both lighter and heavier variations of this type, and some of each lasted until the end.

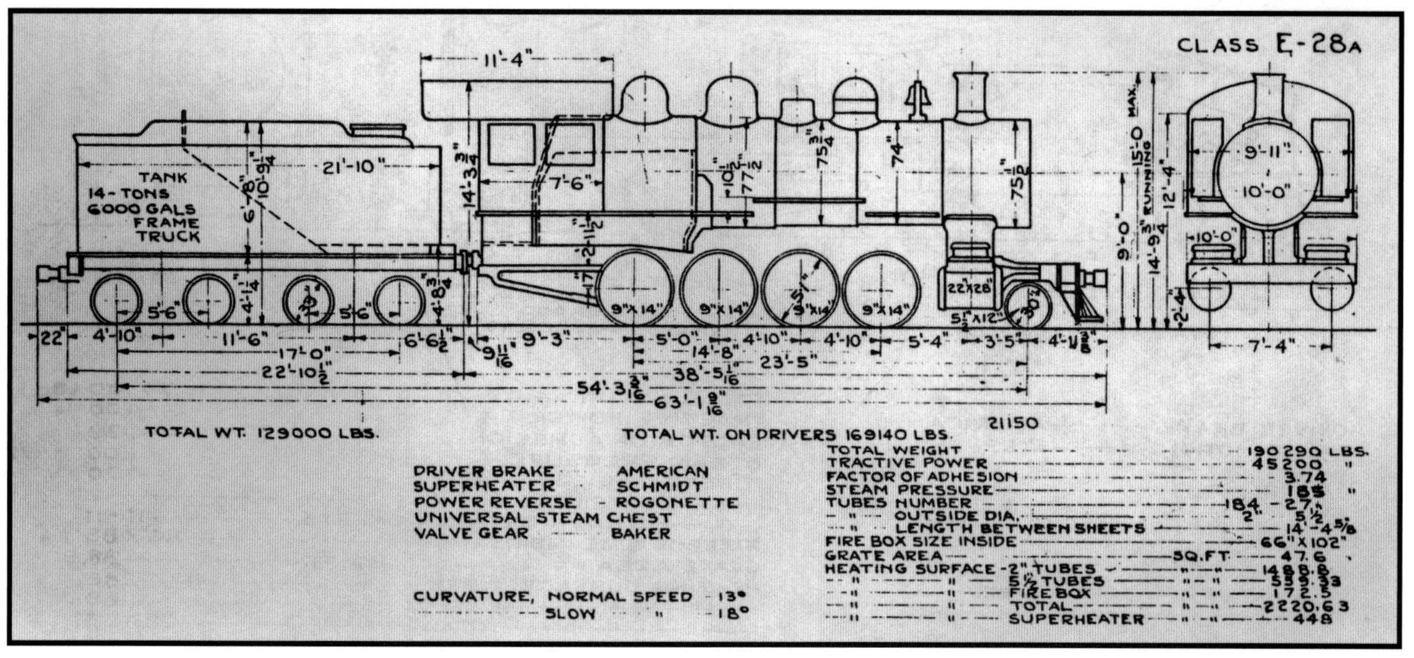

(below) E-19a #1888, one of the many camelbacks owned by the B&O, is captured while awaiting her next assignment on a boring day in Baltimore, on April 16, 1916. She was built in 1900, and features an oil headlight. The engineer, reading a newspaper in the cab to pass the time, might possibly be trying to pick a horse in the fifth race at nearby Pimlico.

(Joseph Lavelle photo)

(above) E-8-60 #1212, built by Baldwin in 1892, pauses at Kenova, West Virginia, in January, 1938. Note the early electric headlight and (practically out of view) the baggage car.

(Leonard W. Rice collection)

(below) In another early view, this time from the fireman's side of the engine, a similar Consolidation, #1266, is seen at the coaling station in Brunswick. She was built by Richmond in 1896.

(Bruce D. Fales photo)

(above) Consolidation #430, sporting an old number, sits in a large, but unknown yard, with a full bunker of coal and a clean stack.

(Leonard W. Rice collection)

(below) E-39 #589, also with an old number, is found at Keyser, West Virginia, on June 11, 1945. Credit the photographer for capturing this view at the height of World War II, when security was tight around railroad facilities. Note the single air pump on the engine, which was built in 1903.

(W. R. Hicks photo)

(above) E-19a #1899 looks tired and forlorn in the Baltimore scrap line, on November 12, 1931. She was built by Baldwin in 1901, as a compound with a conventional boiler. In 1905, just a few years later, the 2-8-0 was converted into a camelback with a Wootten firebox.

(Bruce D. Fales photo)

(above right) E-13 #1639 sits steaming at an unknown location. Built by Baldwin in 1896, she was later converted to a camelback by the B&O.

(Leonard W. Rice collection)

(center right) E-13b #1631 rests at Staten Island, New York, in 1937. This was another camelback conversion by the line. Note the spark arrester, as well as the very clean look of the engine.

(Ted Gay photo, Leonard W. Rice collection)

(below right) Camelback #1635 was photographed in 1945. Also built by Baldwin in 1896, she underwent conversion in the Mount Clare Shops.

(Leonard W. Rice collection)

1639

1631

1635
BALTIMORE AND OHIO

(above) "Just ignore him, maybe he'll go away," the one crewman might be saying, in this view of E-26 #1599. Seen at Storrs, Ohio, in 1925, the engine features 56-inch drivers and an early electric headlight. Built by Baldwin in 1898, she would be retired by 1936.

(Howard Barr photo)

(below) The scene is Hutchinson, West Virginia, on June 10, 1904, as E-14 #1529, built just a few years before by Baldwin, in 1898, poses for a portrait with everyone in the crew, as well as a few onlookers. Note the oil headlight, as well as the "bobber" caboose.

(Howard Barr photo)

(above) E-18a #1901 is seen at St. George Yard, Staten Island, on August 21, 1921. Built as a compound by Baldwin in 1900, she was converted to a simple by the B&O in 1906.
(Joseph Lavelle photo)

(below) This Consolidation, #1902, seen at Newark, Ohio, in 1925, was built as an E-18 by Baldwin in 1900, then converted by the line and reclassified as an E-18a. Compare #1902 with the engine above. Note the two air pumps on this engine, vs. the single air pump on the other. Note as well, on this one, the sideboards on the tender, the different coal bunker configuration, and the lack of a back-up headlight.
(Leonard W. Rice collection)

2349
BALTIMORE AND OHIO
2349

2247
BALTIMORE AND OHIO

BALTIMORE AND OHIO
2784
2784

(above) E-27ca #2715, along with #2831, slug it out upgrade at Laughlin Junction, Pittsburgh, Pennsylvania, on September 16, 1948. Making matters worse, #2715 is hand-fired, and the fireman, taking a breather in the cab window, is no doubt having a real time of it.

(William P. Price photo, Jay Williams collection)

(above left) E-24 #2449 works a cut of cars at Eckington Yard, in Washington, on June 8, 1925. Note the reinforced cylinder housing.

(Leonard W. Rice photo)

(center left) E-24 #2247 is seen at Newark, Ohio, in 1934. With the cab and its protruding overhang, there are definite hints of a style more akin to the rival PRR. Note the small problem this engine is having: namely, the matter of a derailment.

(Howard Barr photo)

(below left) E-27ca #2784, later to become #207 (as seen in the photo on page 32 of this book), is on this day found in Medina, Ohio, in June, 1955. While blocking a street, the engineer is trying to get the attention of the crewman on the ground.

(John A. Rehor photo, Jay Williams collection)

(above) Few cameramen bothered to take photos of the rear end of steam engines, which is too bad, given the resulting gaps in the historic records today. This company photographer, however, not only captured a superb image of the tender of Consolidation #2718, but framed the scene with a water tower. Taken in Brunswick, on September 11, 1945, the picture also shows a charming coupe off to the side.

(B&O photo)

(above right) E-27c #2725 rests under the shadow of an overpass in Grafton, on September 30, 1947. The tender is topped off, and the engine looks ready to find her train and leave town.

(Howard N. Barr photo)

(center right) Consolidation #2872 basks in the Indian Summer sun at Brunswick, on September 22, 1946, in this detail-rich side view.

(Leonard W. Rice photo)

(below right) E-27da #227, formerly #2695 before the big renumbering in 1956, is seen at Zanesville, Ohio, in 1957. The photographer was a faithful fan who captured thousands of images of B&O motive power in southern Ohio.

(Paul Dunn photo, Thomas W. Dixon, Jr. collection)

2725
BALTIMORE AND OHIO

BALTIMORE AND OHIO
2872

227

7 MIKADOS

(above) Mikado #4431, later #419, blasts out of Camden Station, in Baltimore, with train #81. She is passing under a set of hanging "telltales"—a low-clearance warning.
(Leonard W. Rice collection)

"Mikes" complimented 2-8-0s in freight service on the B&O, but were always reserved for prime assignments. They were also far more versatile, being used in passenger service, with a few outfitted with steam heat and train signal equipment.

Perhaps the most versatile type of engine on the line, they were used for fast freights, passenger trains, pusher service in the mountains, and even locals when truly necessary. They were also often double-headed. Given this wide-ranging utility, 2-8-2s lasted until the very end, and a proud Mike headed up the official last steam run.

Unlike the 2-8-0s, which were mainly hand-fired, the newer 2-8-2s had mechanical stokers. There was some experimentation with this type as well, including use of smoke deflectors (or "elephant" ears), special feedwater heaters, and even multi-port exhaust stacks.

The 500-plus Mikados were assigned the Q class, and were numbered in the 4000-4800s.

Their history is linked with military matters. Some, the 4500s, were built as USRA-engines when the government was running railroads during World War I. During the next war, the type name, with its Japanese overtones, was suppressed in an early application of the now *dreaded* political correctness. They were instead called MacArthurs, even MacAdoos, for obvious reasons.

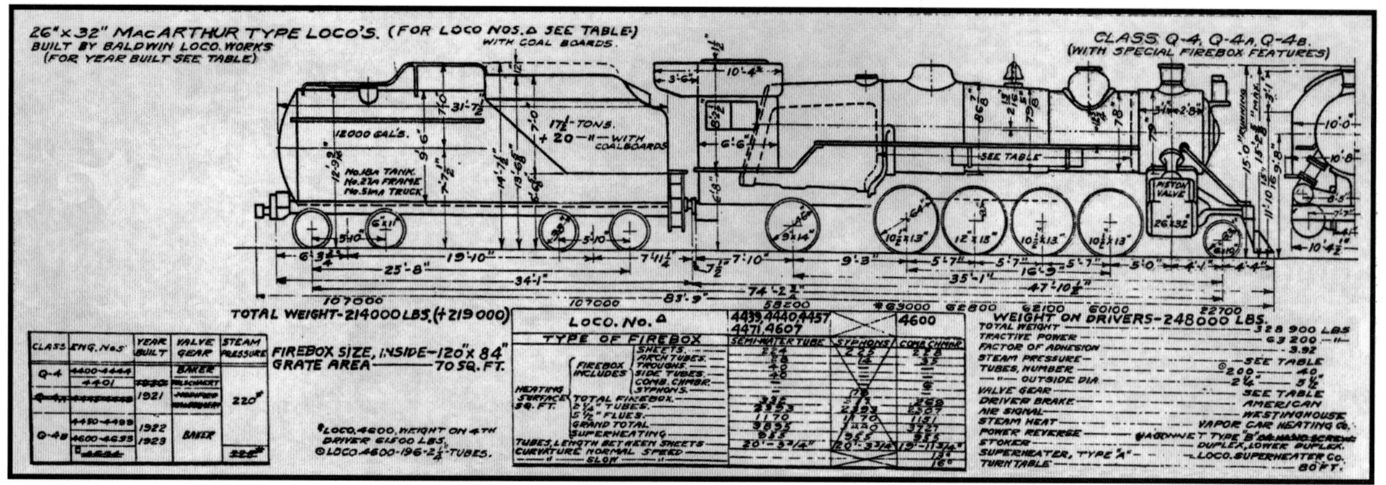

(below) Echoing thunder must fill the confined surrounding area as Q-4 #4459 and a double-heading Pacific P-1 blast through with passenger train #30 (with six head-end cars alone in view), near Kingswood Tunnel, West Virginia. The time is August, 1949, in this priceless view where you can almost smell the coal smoke, steam, and creosote.

(Bruce D. Fales photo, Jay Williams collection)

(above) Q-1c #4299 poses in Philadelphia, in 1933, in this great atmosphere shot taken during the height of the Great Depression. Notice the manual lever reverse on the engine, which would be scrapped in December, 1947.

(Leonard W. Rice collection)

(above right) Mikado #4132 is seen in Washington, during the late 1930s. Built by Baldwin in 1911, she featured a cross-compound air compressor, and would be scrapped in October, 1951.

(Donald A. Somerville photo)

(center right) Q-1 #4132, seen at Potomac Yard, in Washington, on April 10, 1939, was built by Baldwin in 1911. The engine features 24- by 32-inch cylinders and power reverse. Note the very early application of a stack-mounted radio antenna (humor).

(Leonard W. Rice photo)

(below right) Q-1c #4229 is seen in the deadline at Cincinnati. Built by Baldwin in 1913, the big Mike would be scrapped in April, 1952.

(Bruce D. Fales photo)

4132
BALTIMORE AND OHIO

4132
BALTIMORE AND OHIO

4229
RE & OHIO

4320

4473
BALTIMORE AND OHIO

4492
4492

(above) The ground shakes, rattles, and rolls as Q-4 #4445, along with Pacific #5085, roar by the camera location west of Terra Alta, West Virginia, on November 14, 1948. According to the photographer's detailed notes, the train is #30, mostly mail and express, and the time is 10:33 a.m. The 2-8-2 was built by Baldwin in April, 1921, and scrapped in May, 1952.

(Bruce D. Fales photo, Jay Williams collection)

(above left) Engine #4320 sits waiting at Georgetown, Maryland, on June 6, 1948, ready to depart with a "Rail Ramble" fan trip. Note the ex-troop kitchen car, right behind the tender, which has been converted to Railway Express Agency usage.

(Leonard W. Rice photo)

(center left) Q-4b #4473, later to become #449, is seen in Grafton, on October 25, 1955. As noted, the Mikes were extremely versatile. Here, #4473 is double-heading on a west-bound 122-car freight about ready to leave town. Built by Baldwin in 1922, she would be scrapped in December, 1957.

(Leonard W. Rice photo)

(below left) Q-4b #4492 would become #462, and last until the end of steam on the B&O. She is seen here at Brunswick, in 1938.

(Donald A. Somerville photo)

(above) Q-4 #4407 is seen at M & K Junction, West Virginia, on September 28, 1948. This is an early example of using "flashing" to obtain a night-time exposure. The engine was scrapped in November, 1955.

(Bruce D. Fales photo, Jay Williams collection)

(below) In another Chicago scene, we see #4462, later to be #440, in May, 1949. Built by Baldwin in 1922, she would be cut up for scrap in January, 1958.

(Joseph Schmitz collection)

(above) Q-3 #4564, which would become #362, was built by Baldwin in 1918, as a USRA-engine. Seen here, in Charlestown, West Virginia, in July, 1956, she sports steel flags and a full load of coal.

(Joseph Schmitz photo)

(below) Q-3 #4554, a light USRA-engine, would become #352 after the 1956 renumbering, and make it to the end of steam. She had an HT Stoker applied in 1943, and was scrapped in October, 1959. This East St. Louis, Illinois view, from around 1936, was taken by one of the great locomotive portrait photographers.

(R. J. Foster photo, Jay Williams collection)

4603
4603

4628

(above) Q-4b #4628 is captured at one of the all-time classic B&O locations, at Harpers Ferry, West Virginia, on September 24, 1946. She is pulling a 23-car "main" train, a high-priority troop consist. Troop trains *after the war?* Well, how do you think those millions of men got home, after all. Built by Baldwin in 1923, the "MacArthur" would be scrapped in May, 1953.
(Bruce D. Fales photo, Jay Williams collection)

(above left) Q-4 #4603, later #469, is seen at Brunswick.
(Bruce D. Fales photo)

(center left) Q-4b #4628 features a road pilot vs. the usual foot boards, and carried 225 pounds of boiler pressure. She is seen at Potomac Yard, in Washington, on May 1, 1937.
(Leonard W. Rice photo)

(below left) Q4-b #4615 was captured in Baltimore, on July 9, 1944. Just a month after D-Day, this photographer definitely took his chances with the railroad police. And, it was well worth it, for the scene takes in two Mikes (er, sorry, that would be "MacAdoos"), a wooden caboose, and an elegant roundhouse.
(Leonard W. Rice photo)

4858

4837
BALTIMORE AND OHIO

333

(above) It is 5:30 p.m., on May 17, 1958, and history is being made by Q-4 #421, formerly #4434, as it heads north-bound on its return to Cleveland, at Beach City, Ohio. Do we really need to say more? After making the last "official" steam run on the B&O, the proud engine would—alas—be scrapped in November, 1959. Rest in Peace.

(Bruce D. Fales photo, Jay Williams collection)

(above left) Q-7f #4858 is seen at Bayview, Maryland, on June 25, 1939, behind a wooden caboose. She was built by Baldwin in 1916.

(W. R. Hicks photo)

(center left) Q-7f #4837 poses for her builder's photo at the Mount Clare Shops, in 1927. The proud engine featured 64-inch drivers and an oil headlight.

(B&O photo)

(below left) Q-3 #333, #4534 before 1956, is seen at Holloway, Ohio, in July, 1957, not too far along from her demise. Featuring a high-capacity Vanderbilt tender, she was scrapped in January, 1958.

(John A. Rehor photo)

(above) Y #6500 was built by Brooks in 1907, and came to the B&O with the BR&P acquisition on January 1, 1932. With the former owner, the locomotive was #501. She had 52-inch drivers.

(Leonard W. Rice collection)

8 DECAPODS

All the engines of this type, 2-10-0s, that were owned by the B&O, came along with the acquisition of the BR&P. The hulking monsters had been built by Brooks, during the period 1907-1909.

Their type name came from the Latin language (i.e., ten wheels). They were assigned the Y class, and numbered in the 6500s.

While these engines were extremely powerful, given their low driving wheels, they were also very slow, *too slow*, and were quickly forced off the busy main lines as a result.

Given the limited turning radius imposed by their five sets of drivers, their potential use on branch lines was also limited.

As a result, these awesome-looking engines were retired by the early 1950s.

(above) A nice intimate view of the drivers and running gear of Y #6507 is offered in this photo, taken at Riker Yard, Punxsutawney, Pennsylvania (home of the famous groundhog), in September, 1947. The equally famous town is on the mainline of the former BR&P.

(R. Van Boven photo)

(below) Another view of the same engine, #6507, is shown below, a few years later, at an unknown location. No matter the place, or date, the forlorn look of the Decapod tells it all. It is stored unserviceable, with parts missing, and quite ready for the scrapper's torch.

(Leonard W. Rice collection)

9 SANTA FES

(above) The location is Hancock, Maryland, on September 18, 1946, and S-1 #6117 muscles her way along with a heavy load of east-bound coal hoppers. She would survive the 1956 renumbering, becoming #505, and make it to the end of steam, but not beyond that. Sitting on the yard tracks is an ex-Buffalo & Susquehanna (B&S) 2-8-0.

(Bruce D. Fales photo, Jay Williams collection)

The 2-10-2s, popular with B&O crews, were fondly called "Big Sixes" by them (after the number range of the huge engines). With the locomotive's appearance one of massive proportions, the nickname truly fit.

The type itself was first introduced on the Atchison, Topeka & Santa Fe Railway, hence *that* name.

They were assigned the S class, and were numbered in the 6000-6200s (i.e., the "Sixes").

There were two separate incarnations of this type on the B&O, with varying success.

The first included the original S class, over 30 engines built by Baldwin in 1914. They proved much too slow, however, and were withdrawn from service (with two converted to 0-10-0 switchers).

The S-1 class, built by both Baldwin and Lima during 1923-1926, included 125 units, and proved highly effective, combining exceptional power with adequate speed. They were heavily used on the Cumberland, Akron, and Toledo Divisions, where they pulled tremendous loads (ah, but the Big Sixes truly inspired the use of adjectives!).

Even with the success of the newer class of Santa Fes, the B&O mechanical people at the Mount Clare Shops still tinkered with them, making improvements in the 1940s, including front-mounted air pumps.

These engines, *of course*, lasted until the very end of steam.

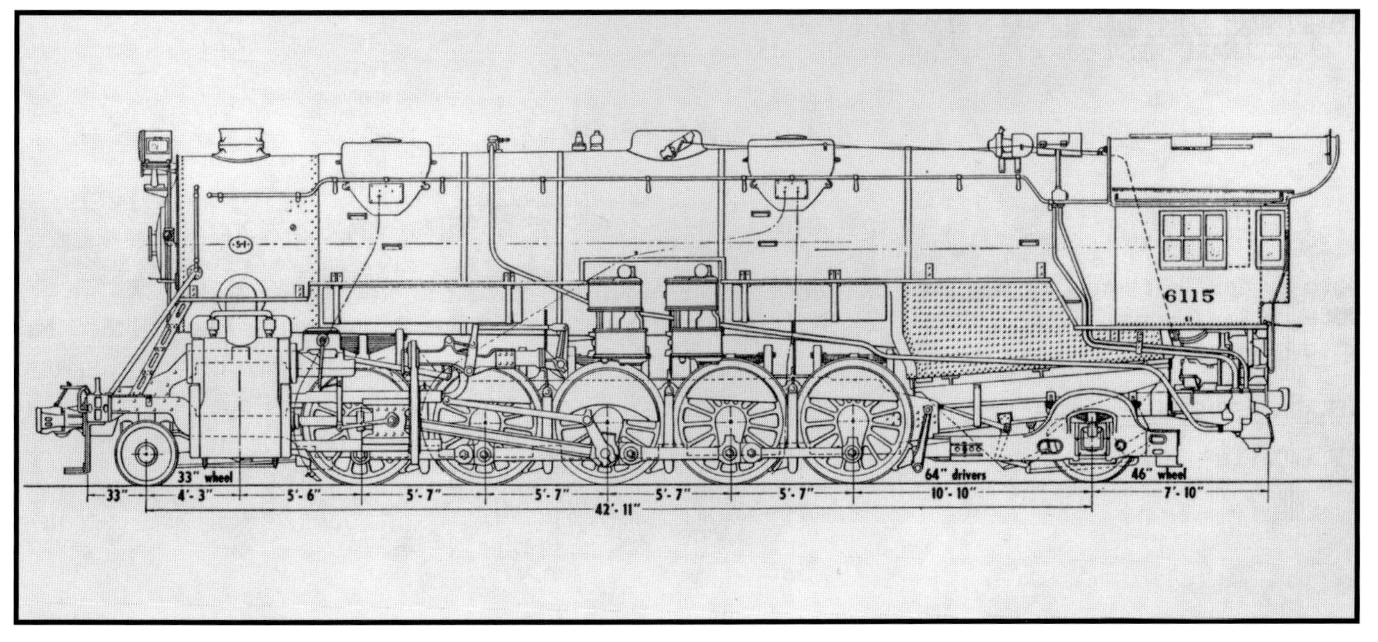

(below) The date is October 17, 1947, and S-1 #6101 is approaching AD Tower, in Orleans Road, West Virginia. The S-1, built by Baldwin, is man-handling (as it was designed to do) an east-bound load of mixed freight.

(Bruce D. Fales photo, Jay Williams collection)

(above) One just had to love the power of the S-1 locomotives. Here, #6120, which became #507 in 1956, pours on the steam and sand as it negotiates the switches and leaves town with an extra freight. The engineer is pulling back on the throttle even more, as his crewmate is trying to figure out what's going on with the camera and all.

(John A. Rehor photo)

(above right) Here, we see S-1 #6162 taking water, in Cumberland, Maryland, on June 8, 1945. She was built by Lima, in June, 1924, and came equipped with dual air compressors for use with long trains and heavy grades.

(W. R. Hicks photo)

(center right) Yet another S-1 poses for the camera, this time #6152, in Brunswick, on July 22, 1950. After 1956, she would be #517.

(Leonard W. Rice collection)

(below right) Santa Fe #6137 (soon to be #512) is seen at New Castle, in December, 1955. She is equipped with an extended tender, with four-wheel trucks.

(Joseph Schmitz collection)

6162
6162

6152

6137
BALTIMORE AND OHIO

6141
6141
6141

6130

6109

(above) S-1 #6100, the very first of a fine group, thunders by with a load of coal hoppers, at an unknown location, but no doubt in mountain country.
(Railroad Avenue Enterprises collection)

(above left) Equipped with a manual lever reverse, "Big Six" #6141 is seen here, waiting for her next assignment. The 2-10-2 was built by Baldwin in 1924.
(Bruce D. Fales photo)

(center left) Another Baldwin S-1, #6130, is seen in Brunswick. Note the difference between this engine and #6141 above: this one is equipped with a running board ladder, vs. steps.
(Leonard W. Rice photo)

(below left) Sitting in sight of the huge coaling tower at Cumberland, in 1938, S-1 #6109 is ready with a full load of coal and steam.
(Bruce D. Fales photo)

(above) A crewman carefully checks out the train on the curve behind them, as S-1a #6209 rumbles through Williamsport, Maryland, on April 17, 1938. The engine is pulling 92 cars east-bound on Western Maryland trackage, but not complaining. Note the open ice hatches on the reefer car behind the tender.

(Bruce D. Fales photo, Jay Williams collection)

(above right) One of the original, slower, and thus less effective S class of engines, #6024 is seen here at the servicing facilities in Brunswick, in war-time 1942. Built by Baldwin in 1914, all of these first 2-10-2s were retired by 1953. Note the slightly different headlight position on this engine.

(Bruce D. Fales photo)

(center right) Here we see the first S-1 again, #6100, this time in Brunswick, on July 22, 1950. The engine was equipped with 64-inch drivers and, in this photo, features an extended-length tender (with the usual six-wheel trucks). Compare the headlight positions of the three engines shown on this page: each is different.

(Leonard W. Rice collection)

(below right) S-1b #6222, which would become #538, poses at New Castle, on July 21, 1954.

(Thomas W. Dixon, Jr. collection)

6024

6100

6222

(above) In an intimate, close-up action view, S-la #6204 is seen passing NO Tower, in Cumberland, in 1945. The big Baldwin was built in 1926.

(Bruce D. Fales photo)

(above right) In a pastoral setting, S-1a #6207 is seen just one mile west of State Line, Pennsylvania, on the Pittsburgh Division. The date is March 13, 1946. Ten years later, the engine would become #534.

(William P. Price photo)

(below right) S-1a #6181 charges west-bound out of the tunnel at Harpers Ferry, in 1948. She was built by Lima in 1926

(Bruce D. Fales photo)

(above) Sporting 78-inch drivers, 4-4-0 #857 sits in Washington, on May 4, 1913. The engineer is about to apply a little lubricant to the running gear, once he figures out what is going on in back of the engine. Meanwhile, the fireman pours on the water.
(Karl E. Schlachter photo)

10 AMERICANS

The 4-4-0s seemed to be practically *the* engine of the B&O in the later part of the 19th Century, from about the 1850s, to the advent of the 4-6-0s. The Americans were used for virtually all passenger trains on the line, as well as some freights. What with their high drivers and very fast speed, they were the engine of choice on the crack express trains.

Unfortunately, they lacked power to match their speed, and were soon replaced, by both 4-6-0s and 4-4-2s (which were in turn soon replaced by the even better 4-6-2s).

Most of the 4-4-0s left the company's roster early on, and by the time of the Great Depression, all but a few were gone.

These elegant, if small engines were assigned several classes over their long life with the railroad, but during the modern era, were kept to the G, H, and M classes, and numbered in the 600-800s.

The Americans had a really nice, clean look at first, but this was certainly due to the simplicity of their functional design. Later, as a variety of different appliances and associated piping were added, the simple look quickly gave way.

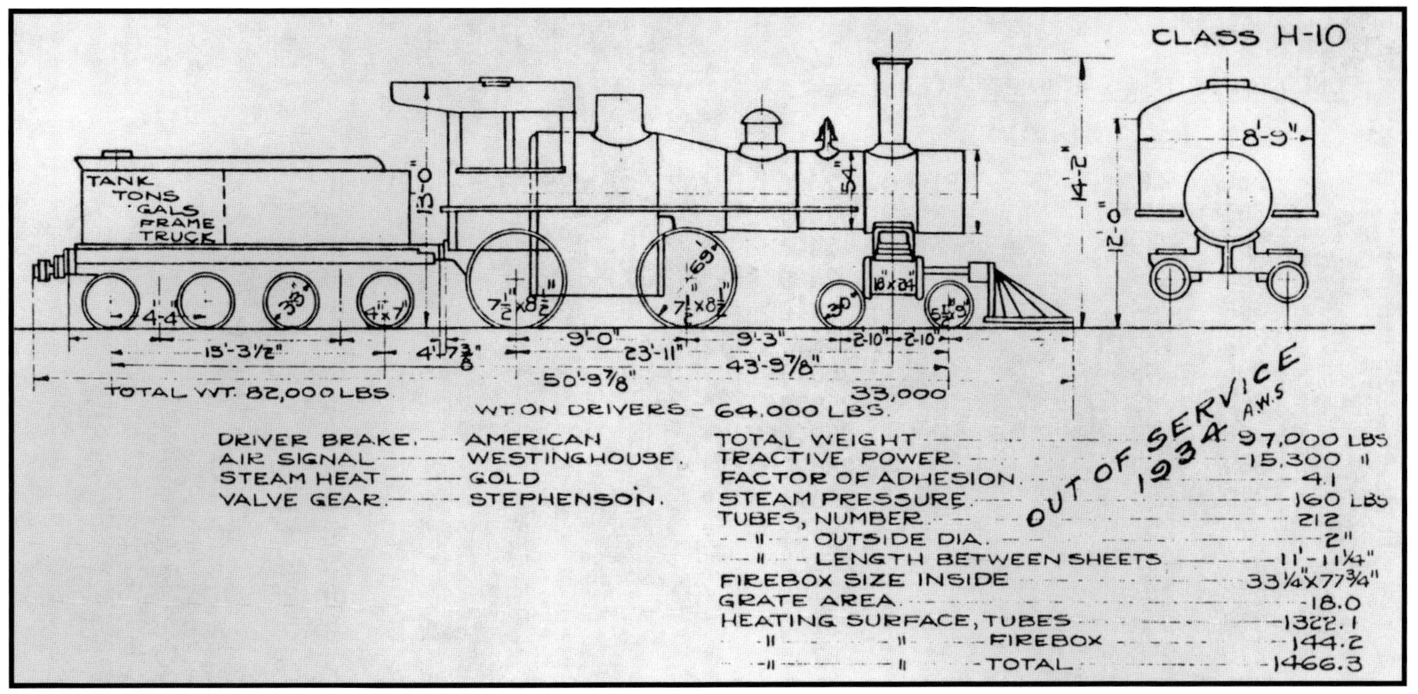

(below) If the engineer in the cab of #859 seems a little proud, even cocky, it is because he is running the engine called "Director General" on this day. Seen in Washington, in January, 1916, the engine is equipped with 78-inch drivers and an oil headlight. Built by Baldwin in 1893 as a compound, it was later rebuilt as a simple. As the famous engine's retirement neared, there was thought given to preservation. It succumbed, however, to the needs of a major scrap drive.
(Karl E. Schlachter photo)

(above) A-3 #1446 sits, ready and waiting, in Mount Clare Yard, Baltimore, in 1935. This company view offers a nice view of both the rear of the engine and tender, and one from above, as well. *(B&O photo)*

11 ATLANTICS

The 4-4-2s which, along with the 4-6-0s, supplanted the 4-4-0s in mainline passenger service in the 19th Century, were in turn replaced by what came to be the ultimate B&O passenger engine—the 4-6-2s.

Still, despite being bumped from the major trains, the Atlantics survived until fairly late in the game for steam on the line. The more modern engines remained on the roster until the mid-1940s, pulling locals and branch-line trains, of course.

While more than half of these fast engines were purchased from Baldwin, a few came along with the acquisition of the BR&P, as well as the B&S.

The fifty-plus engines on the modern roster were assigned the A class, and numbered in the 1400s.

(above) Here is another A-3, #1445, seen from the fireman's side, in 1935. Built by Baldwin in 1910, the 4-4-2s came equipped with 74-inch drivers. The last engines from the class would be retired by 1944.

(Bruce D. Fales photo)

(below) A-3 #1436 is shown on the ready track at Hagerstown, Maryland, in 1938. Note what looks like a speedometer on the trailing truck.

(Bruce D. Fales photo)

(above) In what might be termed 'strictly a lady's thing', J-1 #1, *the Lady Baltimore*, waltzes into Union Station, in St. Louis, Missouri, with *the Ann Rutledge*. The date is September 17, 1937, and the time is—precisely—1:45 p.m. The elegant 4-4-4, later to be #5330 (minus *the name*), was built by Mount Clare Shops in 1934, had 84-inch drivers, and was scrapped in 1949.
(Bruce D. Fales photo, Jay Williams collection)

12 JUBILEES AND HUDSONS

The Jubilees (4-4-4s), and Hudsons (4-6-4s), both represented major experiments on the B&O. The 4-4-4s, of course, never really caught on in America, which went instead with the more powerful 4-6-4s. Both were developed at about the same time.

Rival NYC went with the 4-6-4s in a big way, while the B&O, like the PRR, cast its fate with Pacifics. Both of the latter lines stuck with their large fleets of 4-6-2s right up into the diesel era.

The one Jubliee on the B&O was assigned class J, and numbered 1. The four Hudsons were assigned class V, and numbered 2 (later 5340), 5047, 5350, and 5360. All left the roster by 1950.

One of the Hudsons was named, as well as numbered, and called the "Lord Baltimore." The Jubilee, in turn, was called the "Lady Baltimore."

These two engines were designed with a very clean, uncluttered, *British*-exterior look. Assigned to the prestigious Royal Blue trains between New York and Washington, they created a major media sensation. After the interest waned, however, they proved more style than substance, were relegated to the subsidiary Alton Railroad, then returned home, divested of their semi-streamling, and finally—alas—scrapped!

(above) V-1 #5047 poses at an unknown location. The wires and PRR GG-1 in the background, however, strongly suggest Washington. This beauty was built by Mount Clare in 1933, from the body of a 4-6-2, and featured an experimental water-tube firebox. She was scrapped in 1950.

(Bruce D. Fales photo)

(below) V-3 #5350 poses in Makoringtown, Pennsylvania, in April, 1939. Built by Mount Clare in 1935, she also features the long-running (on the B&O) experimental water-tube firebox. In this view, we can clearly see the British-look of the front of the Hudson.

(Joseph Schmitz collection)

13 TEN-WHEELERS

(above) "Here's looking at you." B-18c poses for the camera at the East Side Yards, in Philadelphia, on June 6, 1937. She was built by Rhode Island, in 1901.

(Leonard W. Rice collection)

The 4-6-0s on the B&O, as noted earlier, helped replace the earlier 4-4-0s in the 19th Century, especially in passenger service. When the Ten-Wheelers, in turn, were eclipsed by the 4-6-2s in that same area of work, at least on the mainline, their primary use quickly shifted to both light-freight and passenger service, but on the railroad's many branch lines.

They were assigned class B, and numbered in the 100s, 1300s, and 2000s.

While there were only about 100 of this type on the B&O, it was one of the more common types of steamers across both the United States and Canada and, during the later part of the 19th Century and the first part of the next one, was one of the most *important* types.

Back on the B&O, this type did not get the respect they deserved: most of them left the roster by the 1940s, with the remaining few departing in the early 1950s.

They were respected by one B&O man, however—Dan Willard, the long-time President. Even though he had favored the equally fast but more powerful Pacifics over the Ten-Wheelers, he had one favorite 4-6-0 painted, with striping and colorful trim reserved for the President class *alone*. That that one engine received overly generous respect and attention from crews may have been due to it being generally referred to as "Dan Willard's engine!"

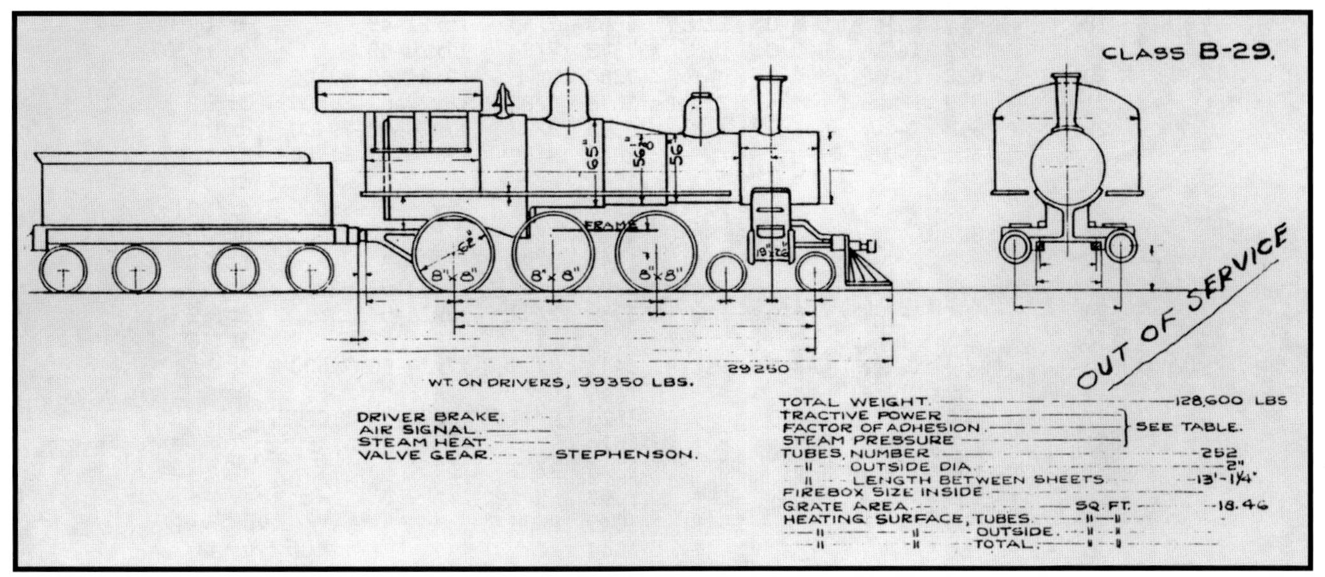

(below) In a scene which had been played out so many times in so many small towns across America, Ten-Wheeler #2042 eases into Marietta, Ohio, in January, 1946, with local train #55. While the fireman is obviously shouting something to the people in the car, we would like to know for sure what is trailing the first coach: a doodlebug?
(Karl E. Schlachter photo)

(above) B-17a #1331 comes flying at us, pulling train #6, in Landsdowne, Maryland, on August 5, 1913. Built by Baldwin in 1901, as a compound, and with 78-inch drivers, she was converted to simple in 1905, and scrapped in 1935.
(Charles B. Chaney photo)

(above right) Ten-Wheeler #1383, built by Baldwin in 1893, is seen on a double-headed freight extra at an unknown location. Note the oil headlight.
(Leonard W. Rice collection)

(center right) A cousin to the above 4-6-0, #1375, also built by Baldwin in 1893, is seen in Baltimore, in 1915.
(Karl E. Schlachter photo)

(below right) Captured at Parkersburg, West Virginia, on October 1, 1949, #1352 had 60-inch drivers, and was built by the Mount Clare Shops in 1891.
(Thomas W. Dixon, Jr. collection)

1375
BALTIMORE AND OHIO

1352
1352
1352
BALTIMORE AND OHIO

2014
BALTIMORE AND OHIO
2014

2012
2012
BALTIMORE AND OHIO

BALTIMORE AND OHIO
2024

(above) B-18 #2022 sits waiting with a freight at Chester, Pennsylvania, in 1920. She was built by Rhode Island in 1901.

(Tom Batesman photo)

(above left) B-18 #2014 was originally built by Rhode Island as a compound, with 68-inch drivers. When converted to simple by the B&O, she was reassigned to class B-18c. She is seen here at an unknown location, on March 17, 1940.

(Howard N. Barr photo)

(center left) B-18c #2012 is shown at Cumberland, on July 5, 1938.

(Bruce D. Fales photo)

(below left) Ten-Wheeler #2024, a B-18ca, poses at Riverside Yard, in Baltimore, in 1927. That said, she not only looks important, but *is* rather important. Commonly referred to as "Dan Willard's engine," the otherwise ordinary engine is decked out with lettering, striping, and trim usually reserved only for *the* President class Pacifics. While she certainly wasn't one of those engines, she had managed to capture and maintain the attention of the top guy. Hence, the special treatment.

(B&O photo)

14 PACIFICS

(above) P-7 #5315, one of the elite *President* class, sits proudly in the roundhouse at Washington, on July 15, 1950. She is equipped with a snow plow-type pilot, but there is surely none of that stuff to worry about on this day.

(Leonard W. Rice photo)

As noted earlier, the fast and powerful (for a passenger engine) 4-6-2s came to be the ultimate in passenger power on the B&O.

Earlier, the line had worked with 4-4-0s, then 4-4-2s and 4-6-0s, in developing their motive power for this type of service. They even experimented with the 4-6-4s, which were highly respected on other roads.

It was in the Pacifics, however, that the road found its ideal match for passenger trains.

They were assigned class P, and numbered in the 5000-5300s, with a few getting streamlining. While the B&O only had about 175 of these engines, they got maximum use and return from their investment, running them until the last year of steam.

Developed and improved over time, the type reached its finest expression in 1927, with the P-7, or "President" class, named for the first 20 Presidents of the United States.

These elegant ladies were the darlings of the railroad, and had the very best classic lines of any American steam locomotive.

They were, in fact, as again noted earlier, the embodiment of the B&O of the era: fast, efficient, and courteous passenger service.

The P-7s, painted green with red and gold trim, the name of a President emblazoned on theirs cabs, said it all. Not the flashiest of engines, they gathered much acclaim for their simply stated grace and beauty.

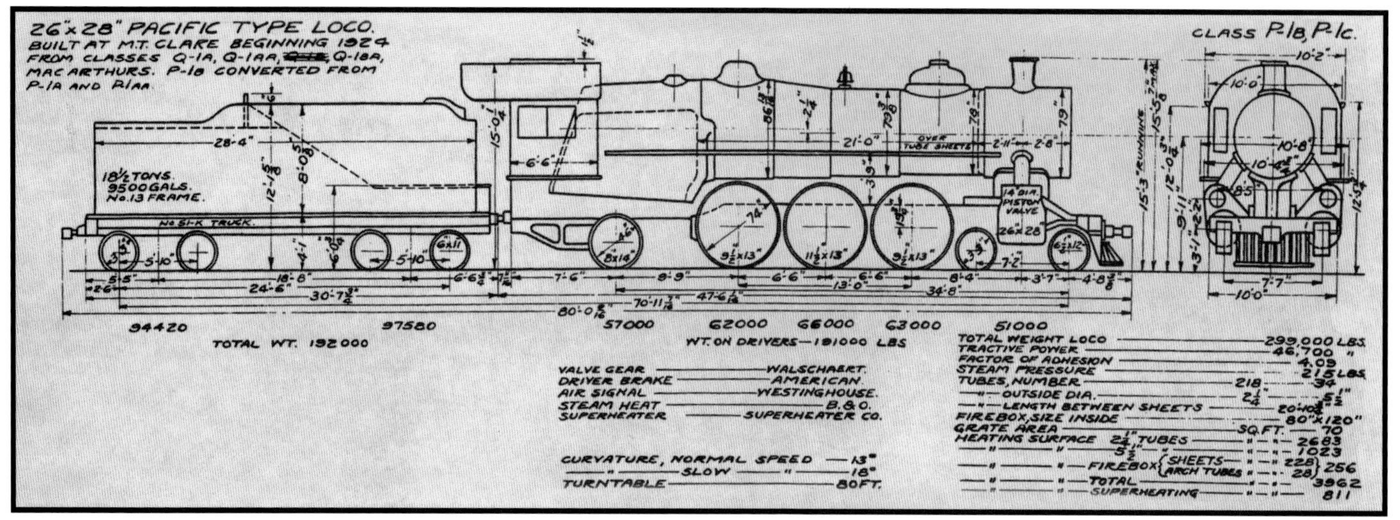

(below) In a scene that speaks so much about the many transitions in American railroading, one of the early Pacifics, P-1d #5049, shares a moment with streamlined President class P-7 #5303, at the service tracks in Cincinnati, in July, 1956. Within weeks, both will have new engine numbers assigned as part of the railroad's effort to deal with the flood of diesels that had come onto the property in recent years. Not long after that, both would start counting the days until the end of steam finally arrived. For the nearly obsolete #5049, which came about when the B&O "rebuilt" her from an out-moded 2-8-2, Q-1 #4120, retirement would come that same year. For #5303, granted a *Presidential* pardon perhaps, it would not occur until ... the very next year. *Alas!*
(Joseph Schmitz collection)

(above) An unidentified Pacific races by as it leaves Silver Spring, Maryland, with its train. Note the tender. First, it is an unusual choice to combine with a 4-6-2. Second, it has a relatively low coal bunker in any case.

(Leonard W. Rice photo)

(above right) P #5033 poses (in that very familiar rods-down fashion), at Storrs, on February 5, 1925. The engine is equipped with two single air pumps, in-board piston valves, and a steel-sheathed snow-plow pilot. Compare the last item with the full-version pilot on the engine shown on page 80.

(Howard Barr photo)

(center right) P-1c #5006 also poses, but beside a gleeming Pennsy GG-1, at Washington, on January 24, 1947.

(Leonard W. Rice photo)

(below right) P-1c #5008, shown here in Washington, only in a fireman's side view, was also "re-built" from the boiler of an unwanted 2-8-2.

(Thomas W. Dixon, Jr. collection)

5033
5033
BALTIMORE AND OHIO

5006
BALTIMORE AND OHIO

5008
5008
BALTIMORE AND OHIO

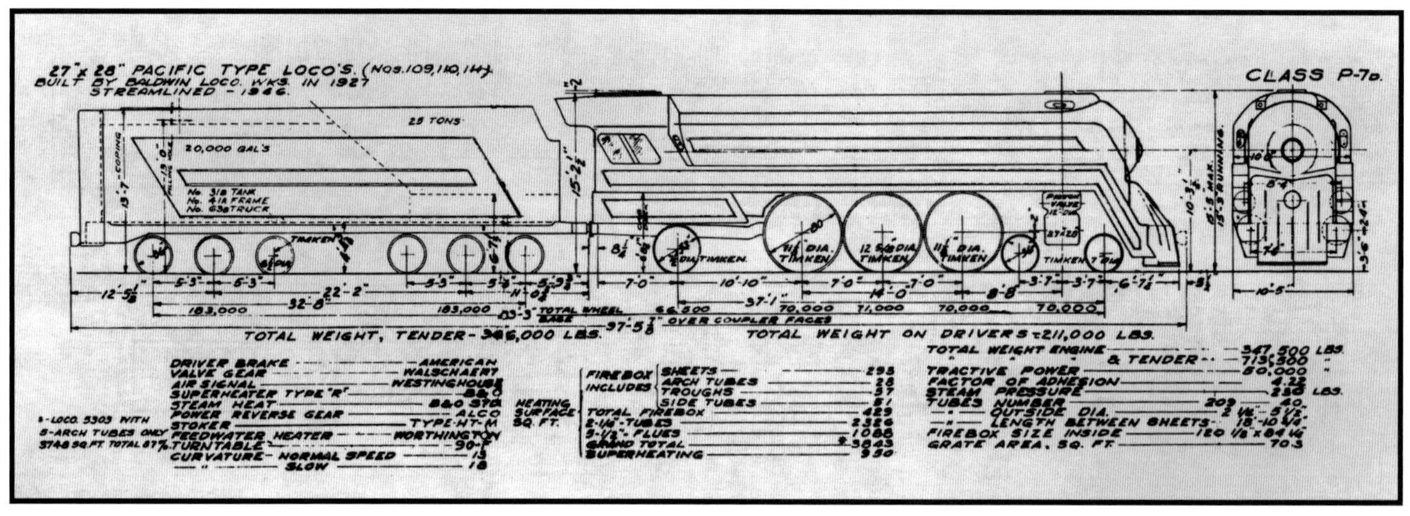

27" x 28" PACIFIC TYPE LOCO'S. (NOS. 109, 110, 14)
BUILT BY BALDWIN LOCO. WKS. IN 1927
STREAMLINED - 1946.
CLASS P-7D.
25 TONS
20,000 GAL'S
No. 318 TANK
No. 41A FRAME
No. 638 TRUCK
TOTAL WEIGHT, TENDER-366,000 LBS.
97'-5 7/8" OVER COUPLER FACES
TOTAL WEIGHT ON DRIVERS=211,000 LBS.
DRIVER BRAKE — AMERICAN
VALVE GEAR — WALSCHAERT
AIR SIGNAL — WESTINGHOUSE
SUPERHEATER TYPE "R" — B&O
STEAM HEAT — B&O STD.
POWER REVERSE GEAR — ALCO
STOKER — TYPE-HT-M
FEEDWATER HEATER — WORTHINGTON
TURNTABLE — 90-F
CURVATURE — NORMAL SPEED — 13
" — SLOW — 18
*-LOCO. 5303 WITH 5-ARCH TUBES ONLY 3748 SQ. FT. TOTAL 87%.
HEATING SURFACE SQ. FT.
FIREBOX INCLUDES SHEETS — 295
ARCH TUBES — 28
TROUGHS — 57
SIDE TUBES — 51
TOTAL FIREBOX — 429
2-1/4"-TUBES — 2326
5-1/2"-FLUES — 1088
GRAND TOTAL — *3843
SUPERHEATING — 950
TOTAL WEIGHT ENGINE — 347,500 LBS.
" " " & TENDER — 713,500 "
TRACTIVE POWER — 50,000 "
FACTOR OF ADHESION — 4.22
STEAM PRESSURE — 230 LBS.
TUBES NUMBER — 209 — 40.
" OUTSIDE DIA. — 2 1/4" — 5 1/2"
" LENGTH BETWEEN SHEETS — 18'-10 3/4"
FIREBOX SIZE INSIDE — 120 1/8 x 84 1/4
GRATE AREA, SQ. FT. — 70.3

5002
BALTIMORE AND OHIO

5038
BALTIMORE AND OHIO

(above) P-1c #5002 comes flying by with speed and a wave of the fireman's hand, kicking up dust and all. This priceless scene is at M & K Junction, on May 15, 1940. The eight-car train is a mail and express run, and the lead car, a coach, may be being used for on-board personnel.
(Bruce D. Fales photo, Jay Williams collection)

(center left) The very same P-1c, #5002, idles away near a large coaling station at an unknown location. Note the switcher in the background above, delivering coal to the station.
(Leonard W. Rice collection)

(below left) Pacific #5038 goes for a ride on the turntable at Grafton, on October 23, 1955.
(Leonard W. Rice photo)

(above) P-3 #5128 pauses, along with local train #62, to take on water for the thirsty engine. The setting is Gauley Junction, West Virginia, in 1946. Built by Baldwin in 1913, the Pacific is no doubt enjoying the last of the final hurrah for steam power.

(Bruce D. Fales photo, Jay Williams collection)

(above right) Another P-3, #5101, is captured in Washington, on February 18, 1948, with an early Southern Railway diesel in the background. The 4-6-2 was built by Baldwin in 1913. Look closely and you will see a rather different type of whistle on the locomotive.

(Leonard W. Rice photo)

(center right) Yet another P-3, this time #5107, is found ready and gleeming at the Mount Clare Shops, in Baltimore, on May 10, 1936. The engine is being prepared for a fan trip. Note the mechanical coal pusher on the tender, immediately behind the top of the coal bunker.

(Leonard W. Rice photo)

(below right) You guessed it, here is one more P-3, #5102, in a perfect rods-down pose, in Washington, on October 12, 1949. These Pacifics had 76-inch drivers, and were fast.

(Leonard W. Rice photo)

5101

5107
BALTIMORE AND OHIO

5102
BALTIMORE AND OHIO
5102

(above) P-5 #5208 is seen at East St. Louis, in September, 1946. The classic pose, as well as sharp focus, are trademarks of this particular photographer.
(R. J. Foster photo, Jay Williams collection)

(right) Pacific #5005 stands for a portrait at Washington, on March 12, 1947. Too many photographers did not take the time to record this part of the engine.
(Leonard W. Rice photo)

(below) P-5 #5220, shown near the coaling tower at Benwood Junction, on April 5, 1956, was built in 1919. The Pacific pulled the last regularly-scheduled steam passenger train into Buffalo, in 1955, and was scrapped in 1956.
(Ed P. Haines photo)

5005
5005
5005
B&O

(above) P-7 #5315 steams through Elizabethport, New Jersey, on the Central Railroad of New Jersey, in June, 1940, with a Washington-Philadelphia-Jersey City express.
(Jay Williams collection)

(above right) Another P-7, #5301, is seen next to yet another GG-1, in Washington, in 1935. She would later be streamlined, assigned to P-7d class and, after 1956, renumbered #109.
(Bruce D. Fales photo)

(center right) Here is still another P-7, #5309, this time seen from the engineer's side. She would become #107 after 1956, and make it to the end of the steam era--but not beyond that.
(Leonard W. Rice photo)

(below right) At the risk of showing too many P-7 engines, we offer #5305, in Washington, *after her re-building*. Compare this Pacific with the two shown above. Note the many changes: the new positions of the bell and headlight, pilot front and hidden air pumps, solid pilot wheels, hidden piping along the side of the boiler, and overall less-cluttered look. In 1956, she would become #105.
(Leonard W. Rice photo)

5301
BALTIMORE AND OHIO

5309
BALTIMORE AND OHIO

5305
BALTIMORE AND OHIO

(above) As the engineer leans far out of the cab to check the track ahead, P-9 #5320 races westbound from Baltimore, past Carroll, Maryland, on June 19, 1929. This particular Pacific, pulling the Capitol Limited, was the sole member of her class, and built by the B&O in 1928. As very evident in the photo, she was equipped with a water-tube firebox.

(Leonard W. Rice photo)

(above right) P-7 #5304 is really *flying* in this photo, as she barely acknowledges passing by Collingdale, Pennsylvania, with the Royal Blue. Sporting the original Loewy-version streamlining in this view, she was later modified with the streamlining configuration shown in the photo below. After 1956, she would take on #111.

(Donald A. Somerville photo)

(below right) Another P-7, #5303 (later to become #110) roars through Grafton, in 1948, with train #76. There are differing views as to which streamlining mode looked best on the President class. The earlier version certainly has that classical, almost Art Decco appeal to it, while the later one has a definite beauty and grace all of its own.

(Bruce D. Fales photo, Jay Williams collection)

15 MOUNTAINS

(above) Ah, but quiet are the times between runs, when the mighty locomotives had to retire for service and repairs. This unidentified 4-8-2 is seen at Willard, Ohio, on May 17, 1956, nestled under the smoke jack.

(Bruce D. Fales photo, Jay Williams collection)

Aside from the EM-1s (or Yellowstones), the 4-8-2s came as close as the B&O managed to to come to having truly modern or "Superpower" steam engines.

The Mountains were assigned class T, and numbered in the 5500-5600s. The line had just over 50 engines of this type.

The first two featured water-tube fireboxes, and were built at Mount Clare. The road bought two more from Baldwin, then built another 40 on its own. Finally, they acquired another dozen or so Baldwin units from the Boston & Maine Railroad (B&M).

The engines were fast and powerful, and handled the important, fast merchandise freights on the line, as well as some of the major passenger trains, especially in the mountain areas. Many featured the latest in steam technology: cast steel frames, roller bearings, and the like

It should be no surprise that they not only made it to the very end of steam, but were one of the last two groups of steam engines to be officially retired (*in 1960*, two years after the official end). No doubt, the ever-frugal and highly cautious motive power officials on the railroad wanted to be absolutely certain the end was really *the end* before letting go of the magnificent engines (some of which were little more than ten-years-old).

The other type of engine in that last group, by the way, were the EM-1s. Does that tell you anything?

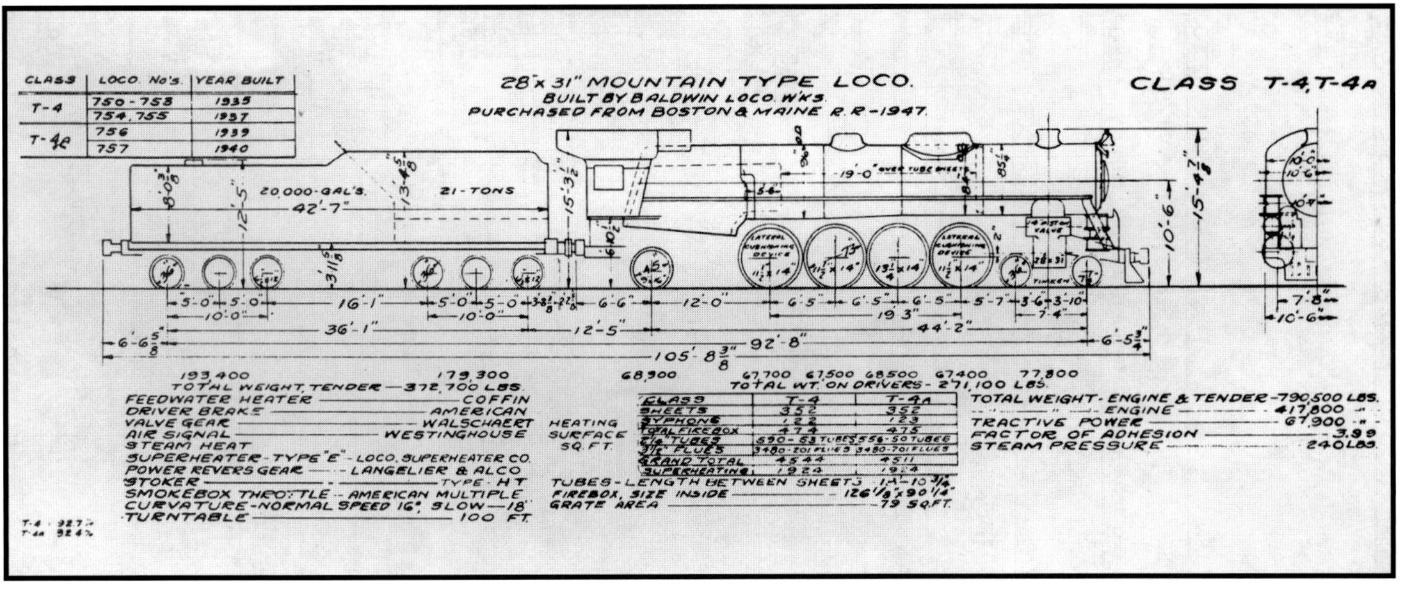

(below) T-3 #5579 rolls—seemingly without much effort—through Hampton, Pennsylvania, on September 17, 1952. Built at the Mount Clare Shops, in 1945, she comes equipped with 70-inch drivers, and is hauling train #21 in this view. After 1956, she would become #721.

(William P. Price photo)

5510
BALTIMORE AND OHIO
5510

5510

5510

(above) T-1 #5510 roars through Georgetown Junction, Maryland, in 1936, with train #6, the Capitol Limited. Built by Baldwin in 1930, she came with 74-inch drivers and a water-tube firebox. Despite her impressive looks, she left the roster by the end of 1951.
(Bruce D. Fales photo, Jay Williams collection)

(above left) Here is #5510 again, this time from the engineer's side. She is seen in Washington, in 1950, coming east-bound off the wye.
(Leonard W. Rice collection)

(center left) In yet another view, we see #5510, this time, as evidenced by the signal bridge, at Union Station, also in Washington. It is July 4, 1930 (Happy Birthday, America!), and the gleaming engine is only a few months old.
(Bruce D. Fales photo)

(below left) Taking one more pass for the photographer, our same #5510 speeds by at an unknown location.
(Leonard W. Rice collection)

5501
TIMO RE & OHIO
5501

(above) T-2 #5550, also featuring a water-tube firebox, was built by Baldwin as well, in 1930, and, like the #5510, was the only member of her class. Unlike the other engine, however, she lasted longer—by *one* year. She is shown here clipping through Silver Spring (notice the blurr on the front of the locomotive), heading into Washington, on July 8, 1938. The photographer's notes, ever so detailed, indicate the train as the Capitol Limited, and the precise time as 7:25 a.m.
(Bruce D. Fales photo, Jay Williams collection)

(above left) Here is #5550 again, only in Rockville, Maryland, on July 5, 1940. She is pulling the Queen City Express.
(Bruce D. Fales photo)

(center left) Mountain #5501—not a T-2, or even a T-1, but one of the original T class—is seen here at the Ivy City roundhouse, in Washington, on July 6, 1945. She was built by the B&O, using the boiler from S-class 2-10-2 #6030, and had 74-inch drivers.
(Leonard W. Rice photo)

(below left) Here is old friend, T-1 #5510, again, only with an extended tender with four-wheel trucks. She is seen steaming away, in a perfect side view at New Castle, on October 29, 1938.
(G. A. Doeright photo)

(above) T-3 #5566, later to become #708, is doing here one of the things she was designed to do: pull long passenger trains at speed. The magnificent machine is working her way through an S-curve, near Myersdale, Pennsylvania, on September 24, 1952.

(William P. Price photo)

(above right) T-3 #5572, later #714, poses here at Blue Island, Illinois, on December 30, 1953. She was built by the Mount Clare Shops in 1944.

(Thomas W. Dixon, Jr. collection)

(center right) It is April 1, 1947, in Curtis Bay, Maryland, and T-3 #5586 (later #727), fresh out of Mount Clare, is on her maiden run with the B&O. The big Mountain had 70-inch drivers.

(Howard N. Barr photo)

(below right) In Fostoria, Ohio, in the late 1950s, hard-working T-3 #5581 surely announces her thundering presence to the local folks. Built by the talented shop crews of the B&O in 1945, she would become #723 in 1956.

(Thomas W. Dixon, Jr. collection)

BALTIMORE AND OHIO

5586

BALTIMORE AND OHIO
5655

5661

BALTIMORE AND OHIO

(above) "So, there was this *traveling salesman*, you see, and a *farmer's daughter*, and ..." Crew members exchange important information before T-4 #753 leaves Willard, in the Spring of 1957. The ex-B&M Mountain was formerly #5654, prior to the 1956 renumbering.
(Robert Hundman photo, Jay Williams collection)

(above left) Another T-4, #5655, also ex-B&M, poses, rods down, at New Castle, in October, 1956. Built by Baldwin during 1935-1940, these engines came with 73-inch drivers.
(Joseph Schmitz collection)

(center left) The 13 T-4 Mountains came to the B&O from the B&M, in 1947, when most of them were ten-years-old, or less. Here, #5661, which will become #756 after 1956, is seen at New Castle, in August, 1957.
(Joseph Schmitz collection)

(below left) Taking a ride on a turntable at an unknown location, 4-8-2 #727 is ready for action with a full load of coal.
(Thomas W. Dixon, Jr. collection)

(above) DD-1 #2400, also known as "Old Maude," proudly poses, with a serene-looking fireman in the cab window, on September 24, 1927. As the first compound Mallet in America, she was a star at the Fair of the Iron Horse, held in Halethorpe (yes, those are actually people sitting in the stands, watching the festivities—those were different times, back then, after all).
(B&O photo)

16 EARLY ARTICULATEDS

0-6-6-0s and 0-8-8-0s

With these two types of engines, and in particular, the former, the B&O pioneered the development of the compound articulated locomotive, commonly called the "Mallet," after its inventor, Anatole Mallet.

The line introduced the concept to American railroads in 1904, with the purchase of "Old Maude," an 0-6-6-0.

The Mallet concept allowed the use of steam twice. It was used first in a set of high-pressure cylinders, and then again in a pair of larger, lower-pressure cylinders, before being exhausted into the atmosphere. It thus squeezed almost twice as much mechanical energy out of the same quantity of steam, using the same amount of coal and water.

The B&O had one 0-6-6-0, which was assigned class DD-1, and numbered 7000. It had 30 0-8-8-0s, assigned to class LL-1, and numbered in the 7000s. Lacking both speed and a leading truck, all of these big engines were assigned to both pusher and hump yard service, and were retired by 1950.

It is interesting to note that Old Maude, #7000, was a *handbomber* (i.e., fired by hand)! If that wasn't bad enough, imagine the poor fireman on a day when the engine was steaming poorly. Heaven help him.

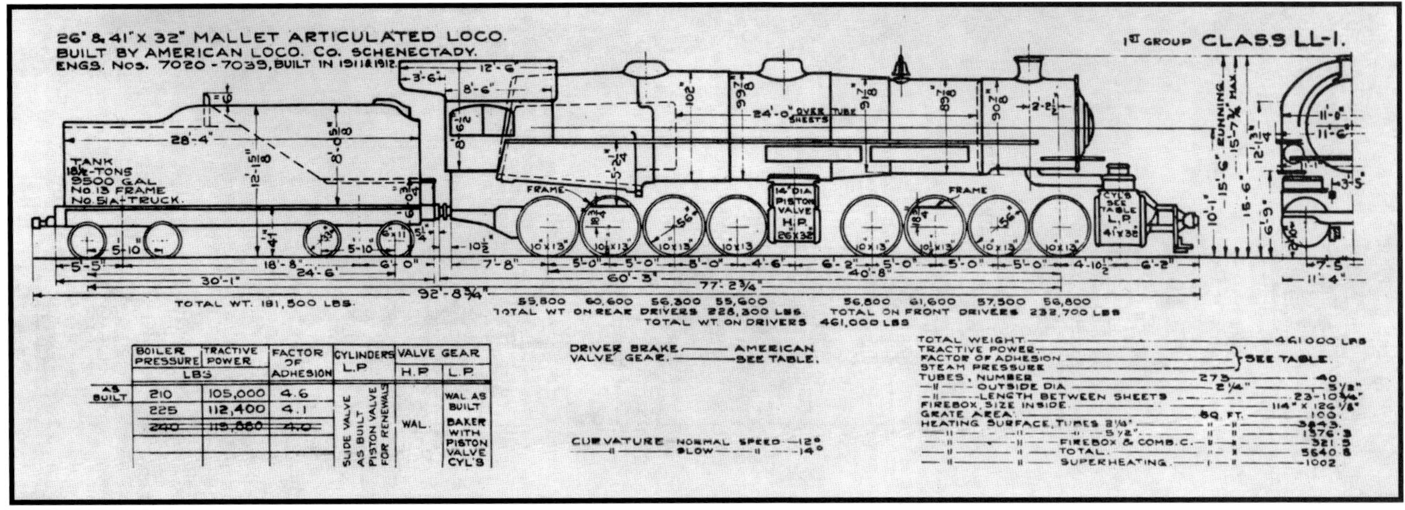

	BOILER PRESSURE	TRACTIVE POWER	FACTOR OF ADHESION	CYLINDERS L.P	VALVE GEAR H.P	VALVE GEAR L.P.
	LBS	LBS				
AS BUILT	210	105,000	4.6	SLIDE VALVE AS BUILT PISTON VALVE FOR RENEWALS	WAL.	WAL AS BUILT
	225	112,400	4.1			BAKER WITH PISTON VALVE CYL'S
	~~240~~	~~119,880~~	~~4.0~~			

(below) "Old Maude" later became #7000, but not in the 1956 renumberings! In the view below, we see the engineer's side. She had been designed by John E. Mulfield, and helped the B&O, as well as other railroads, along on their search for increased power in steam locomotives. As to the earlier comment regarding the engine's one-time star-status, while things were, in fact, different, back in the 1920s, things don't change after all. Being a celebrity in 1927 didn't save her from being scrapped in 1938.

(Donald A. Somerville collection)

(above) KB-1 #7704 sits waiting, even posing, while heading up a coal drag at an unknown location. Especially from this low angle, these engines looked impressive, almost ... intimidating.
(Leonard W. Rice collection)

17 SMALL ARTICULATEDS

2-6-6-2s and 2-6-6-4s

With these two types of engines, the B&O continued its development of the articulated locomotive.

Another great advantage of this kind of motive power was that it placed two engines (i.e., cylinders and driving wheels) under a single boiler, thus a very long boiler could be used. The leading engine simply swiveled under the front of the boiler, allowing the locomotive to negotiate much tighter curves than if the drivers were placed in a rigid frame.

This development allowed for major increases in tractive effort, and was a definite success.

The B&O had over 50 2-6-6-2s, which were assigned to class KK, and numbered in the 7400-7500s. It had only 10 2-6-6-4s, assigned class KB, and numbered in the 7700s. Almost all of the 2-6-6-2s were ex-BR&P engines, while the 2-6-6-4s came to the B&O from the Seaboard Air Line Railroad.

These engines were more successful than the early articulateds, and were used on heavy freight trains, especially in the West Virginia mountains, and on the old BR&P line in Western New York and Pennsylvania. There was an initial attempt at modernization, but the advent of diesels ended further efforts. Some of these engines lasted up until 1953.

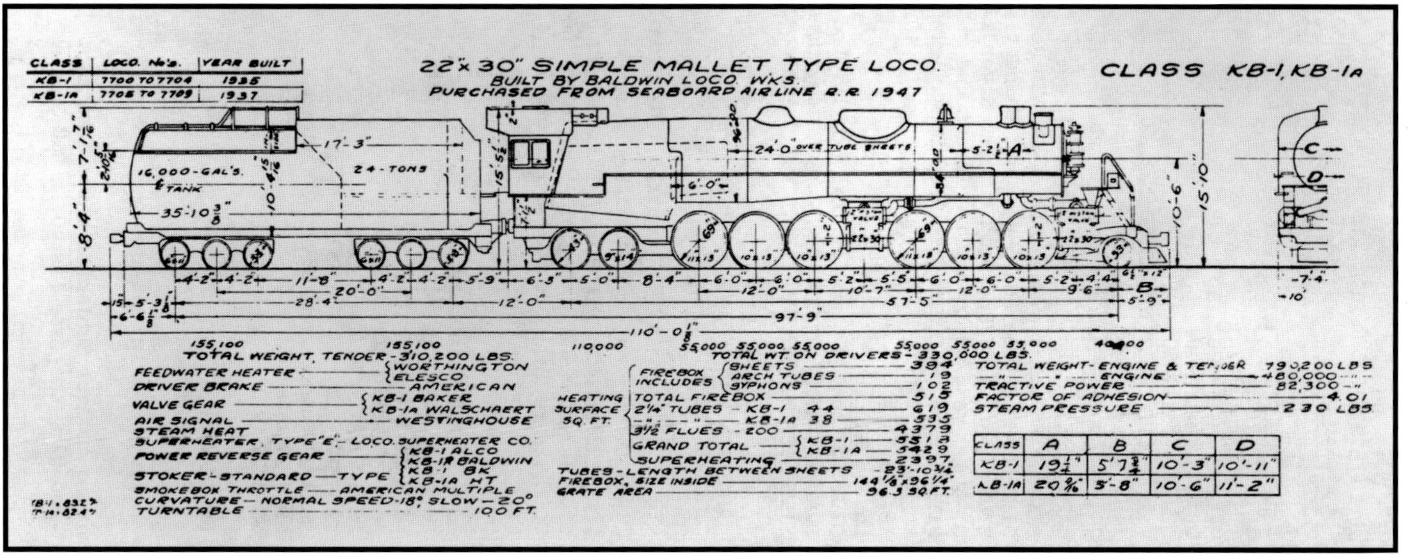

(below) Another KB-1, #7705, is seen at Cumberland, in 1947, in this company view. The front of these locomotives certainly had a *busy* look to them.

(B&O photo)

(above) KK-2 #7450 was the only member of her class. Built by Baldwin in 1930, she was a simple articulated, and is seen here in Cumberland.

(Bruce D. Fales photo)

(below) Here is another view of KB-1 #7704, captured in Keyser, on August 7, 1947. She was acquired second-hand from the Seaboard which, like most deep-southern railroads, did not go in for articulateds in a big way.

(Leonard W. Rice photo)

(above) KK-4 #7543 is seen at Bingham, Pennsylvania, in September, 1949, heading up a freight train. Built by Brooks, in 1923, she came to the B&O along with the BR&P acquisition, and would be retired in 1952. With her former owner, she had been #743. Note the really large low-pressure cylinder housings (which are also reinforced) in front of the engine, as well as the proliferation of lubricators above the high-pressure ones.

(Joseph Schmitz collection)

(below) KB-1 #7707 poses at the Mount Clare Shops, in Baltimore, in 1947. Note the steamboat whistle.

(Leonard W. Rice collection)

(above) EL-5 #7153 slugs it out with a 52-car train of loaded coal hoppers on a grade at Terra Alta, on November 14, 1948. These heavy and powerful Baldwins, built during 1919-1920, would remain on the company roster until 1954.
(Bruce D. Fales photo, Jay Williams collection)

18 LARGE ARTICULATEDS

2-8-8-0s and 2-8-8-2s

The B&O had over 100 2-8-8-0s, which were assigned class EL, and numbered in the 7000-7300s. It had less than ten 2-8-8-2s, assigned to class EE, and numbered 7316-7324. The vast majority of 2-8-8-0s were built by Baldwin, with another ten or so built by the Mount Clare Shops. A similiar number of the same engines were built by Richmond, and were acquired second-hand from the Seaboard. All of the 2-8-8-2s were built by Brooks, and came to the B&O from the BR&P.

Some of the early 2-8-8-0s were compounds, while the later ones were simple. While both types of engines were huge, the compounds had the added element of really *enormous* cylinders, and looked awesome coming around a curve: the cylinders as big as a man, the long boiler veering off to the side.

Most of both types of engines were used in the Pennsylvania and West Virginia mountains, with heavy coal trains. When knocked off the main line by the new diesels, many were transferred to the Indiana Branch (in Pennsylvania), where they continued to haul coal. Some engines from both types lasted on the roster up until 1954.

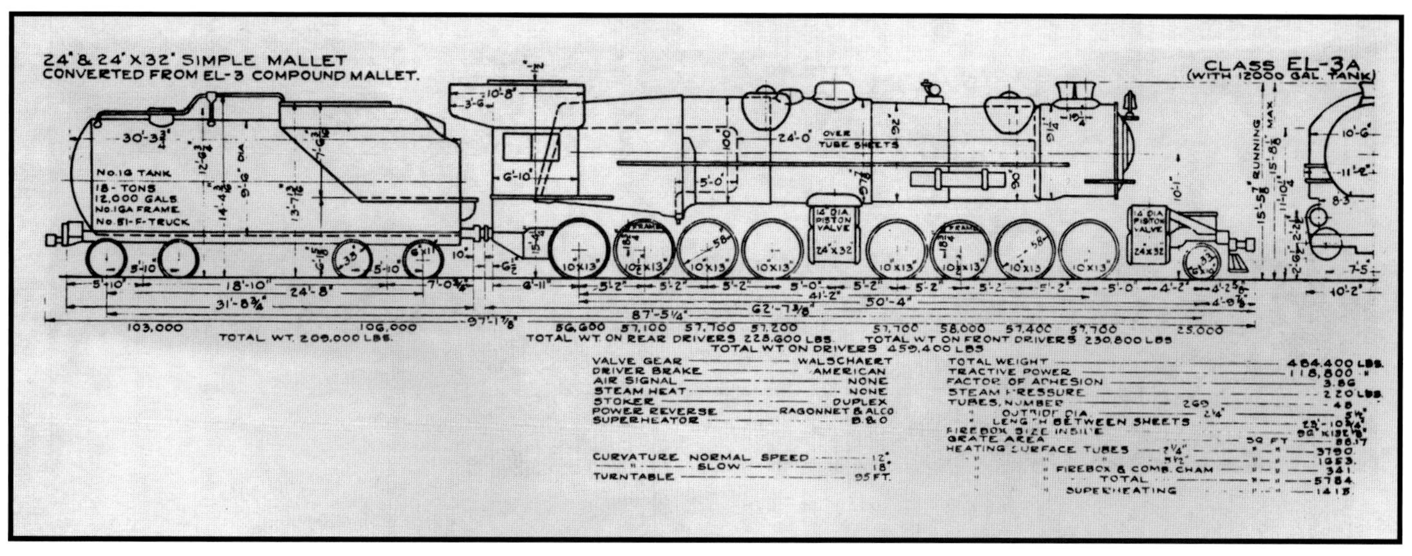

(below) We can almost feel the ground trembling, as we view this EL-2, #7200, powering its way west-bound with a long string of coal hoppers. The big brute is passing K Tower, in Blazer, West Virginia, on October 16, 1947. Built by Baldwin in 1916, she had 58-inch drivers.

(Bruce D. Fales photo, Jay Williams collection)

7119

2033

7141

(above) EL-1 #7114 is seen pounding the rails in Corrigensville, Maryland, on March 13, 1945. Built by Baldwin in 1916, she was the last of her class to roll off the erection floor, and is heading west-bound in this view. Did we mention, by the way, how *huge* those low-pressure cylinders were on these engines?
(William P. Price photo)

(above left) EL-3 #7119, though not of the same class as #7114 above, shows the results of a conversion from compound to simple, especially as regards the size of the forward cylinders. Seen at Cumberland, in 1940, she was built by Baldwin in 1917, and had 58-inch drivers.
(Bruce D. Fales photo)

(center left) EL-4 #7033 was rebuilt from an 0-8-8-0. She is seen at M & K Junction, on September 28, 1948, at 8:30 p.m. While the night-time photography of men like O. Winston Link set the standard in this area, we will always admire the earlier attempts, especially by people working with flash bulbs in a non-synchronized fashion. Well, no matter the technique, the results here were good, and the atmosphere most inviting.
(Bruce D. Fales photo, Jay Williams collection)

(below left) Here is an engineer's-side view of EL-3 #7141, also converted from a compound.
(Bruce D. Fales photo)

(above) This view brings to mind several thoughts: big power, heavy freight, and rugged mountains. EM-1 #7622 is seen charging up Cranberry Grade, near legendary Salt Lick Curve, in West Virginia, heading east-bound, around 1948. After 1956, she would become #672 and, of course, make it to the end of steam—but not beyond.

(Bruce D. Fales photo, Jay Williams collection)

19 YELLOWSTONES

As noted earlier, the 2-8-8-4s, or EM-1s, as they were referred to on the B & O, represented the ultimate in steam technology on the line.

There were 30 engines of this type. All were assigned class EM-1, and numbered 7600-7629. They were built by Baldwin during 1944-1945.

As also noted earlier, the EM-1s were one of the last two types of steam engines to be officially retired by the line (*in 1960*, two years after the official end). As with the Mountains (the other type), the officials in Baltimore wanted to be sure there would be no last traffic surges, etc., before they sent these surperb and relatively new engines to the scrapper's torches.

As an indication of just how satisfied the motive power people were with them, they made no modifications to the powerful giants. At the same time, it has been argued by some that the line under-utilized the EM-1s, by not using them, for example, with fast merchandise freights.

Toward the end of steam, they spent much time handling the heavy coal traffic between New Castle and Painesville.

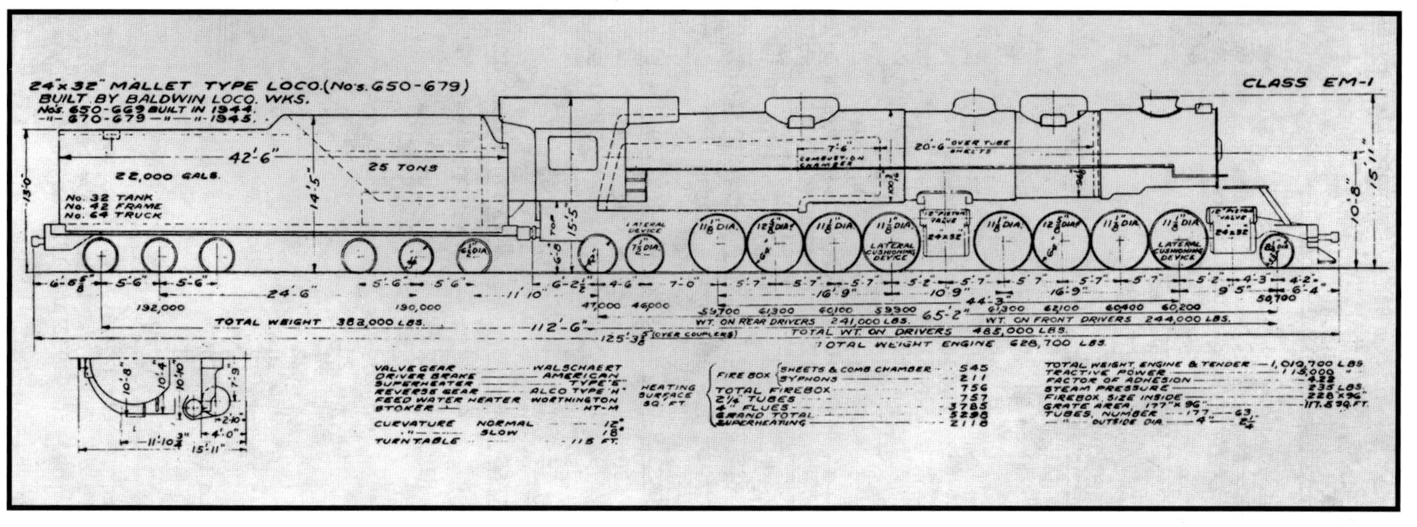

(below) Another one of the *magnificent* EM-1s, #7607, later #657, snakes around a mountain curve, heading west-bound, near Kingswood, on July 27, 1949. In this view, the giant engine looks almost like a brass model.

(Bruce D. Fales photo, Jay Williams collection)

(above) Literally *darkening* the sky overhead, and causing definite ripples in the water flowing beside the tracks, EM-1 #7619 manhandles an east-bound coal train, near Tunnelton, West Virginia, on June 11, 1949. After 1956, she would lose a digit in her number, becoming #669, but not one bit of respect from the railroaders who worked with her.

(Bruce D. Fales photo, Jay Williams collection)

(above right) EM-1 #657, formerly #7607, pours on the coal smoke while just sitting there at Holloway, on November 16, 1957. Given the many fine superlatives attributed to this class of engines, one has to speculate what an *EM-2* would have been like.

(Bruce D. Fales photo, Jay Williams collection)

(center right) Given their size and power, and in particular, their inordinate requirements for generating large masses of thermal energy, the EM-1 locomotives went through coal and water like a bunch of *hungry* locusts tearing through a field of ripe grain. Shown here at the service tracks in Wheeling, West Virginia, in July, 1956, soon-to-be #677 gets her near-insatiable appetite satisfied—for now!

(Joseph Schmitz collection)

(below right) The Yellowstones (by which the EM-1 class was seldomly referred to by B&O men) had 64-inch drivers, which would have let them really open up the throttle on the flat spaces of Ohio and Indiana, if the road would have chosen to allow them to do so. Here, #678, formerly #7628, is seen at Lorain, Ohio, in July, 1957.

(Joseph Schmitz collection)

7627

BALT IMOR

(above) Oh, mother! EM-1 #7620 barrels through Harpers Ferry, on September 24, 1946, with the fireman really pouring the coal to her, as the engineer concentrates on making a run for a nine-mile hill just ahead. The train, manifast #3/97, west-bound for St. Louis, is at HF Tower. The hard-working engine would become #670 after 1956.

(Bruce D. Fales photo, Jay Williams collection)

(above left) "Take this, Hitler!" The very first EM-1, #7600, built by Baldwin, in 1944, is fresh off the factory floor, and already pounding the rails, helping to *feed* the growing American Arsenal of Democracy, with an equally fresh batch of Army tanks. After the war, the veteran work horse went on to become #650.

(B&O photo)

(below left) Here is more evidence that the United States was not going to fail in taking on the Axis powers in World War II. EM-1 #7601, later #651, rolls a long train-load of coal toward the waiting steel mills. She is seen near Cumberland, on March 7, 1944, just three months before the Allies would launch the largest amphibious invasion in the history of the world. Far more ships, built with American steel, took part in this one battle than even existed in the entire combined fleets of the enemy. And recall, we were also conducting major multiple attacks—at the same time—in the Pacific!

(Bruce D. Fales photo, Jay Williams collection)

(above) This view might be appropriately entitled "A Meeting of the Moderns." N-1 #5600, a non-articulated duplex, with the novel water-tube firebox, and British styling, speeds out of Washington, in 1938. On the side is the highly successful GG-1 of the rival Pennsy, which would be the future star of its Washington-New York passenger service. Meanwhile, #5600, built by Mount Clare in 1937, and called the George H. Emerson, after its developer, did not prove anywhere near as successful as the GG-1. It was scrapped by 1950.
(Leonard W. Rice collection)

20 EXPERIMENTALS

The B&O was no doubt among the forefront of American railroads that experimented with their steam motive power. Whether it was building an entirely new engine, as with the 4-4-4-4 duplex; trying out new water-tube firebox systems; or simply modifying feed-water heaters; the officials and crews at the Mount Clare Shops were possessed of great determination.

While this type of work went back to the early days of the line, including efforts to develop the compound Mallet, much of it took place under the direction of George H. Emerson, Chief of Motive Power and Equipment.

The success of all this work varied. Certainly, the Mallets were a hit. On the other hand, the water-tube fireboxes were not. In the latter case, at least, there were repeated attempts made before the towel was thrown in.

It should be noted that not all of these experiments dealt with functional or mechanical issues. In the case of the Lord and Lady Baltimore engines, they involved matters of design. With that experiment too, the results were mixed. While the engines created a media sensation with their fresh look, their performance did not live up to expectations.

(above) Here is another view of #5600, from the fireman's side of the engine. She is seen at the New York World's Fair, in 1939.

(Leonard W. Rice photo)

(below) Another experiment coming from Mount Clare was 4-4-6-4 #7400. She was built in 1932, from a 2-6-6-2, and was equipped with a water-tube firebox and 70-inch drivers. As a measure of her success, she was converted *back* into a 2-6-6-2 in 1933. More effective in that new (or was it old?) form, the articulated lasted until 1953.

(B&O photo)

(above) With consolidation #2504, the line tried out a water-tube firebox, then assigned the engine to class E-27x. She is seen here in Baltimore, in 1927.
(B&O photo)

(below) With another Consolidation, #2722, the B&O experimented with Poppet valves. This engine, seen in Baltimore, in 1927, had 62-inch drivers and was hand-fired. She was scrapped in 1949.
(B&O photo)

(above) This 2-8-2, #4610, seen at Morrell Park, Maryland, on October 30, 1950, looks more like a German engine. The unit features elephant ears and an experimental, European *Kylchap* exhaust system. That last element, installed in 1950, was removed in 1952. As a conventional #474, she survived beyond the 1956 renumberings.

(Howard N. Barr photo)

(below) Another 2-8-2, #4045, was outfitted with both a water-tube firebox, and an experimental feedwater heater. She was assigned class Q-1x.

(Leonard W. Rice collection)

(above) EL-1 #7109 and EL-2 #7202 lend their considerable strength as pushers on this heavy east-bound extra coal drag. The train is seen on Salt Lick Curve, on June 12, 1949, at 11:26 a.m. We can just imagine the thunderous noise echoing through the air.

(Bruce D. Fales photo, Jay Williams collection)

PHOTO GALLERY

(above right) EM-1 #7624, later #674, roars by with an east-bound train on the curve at Rodemor, West Virginia, on September 24, 1948. She is working hard on the grade, with a heavy 52-car train in tow.

(Bruce D. Fales, Jay Williams collection)

(below right) Big Six #6220, an S-1a, is hard at work pushing a freight at Laughlin Junction, in Pittsburgh, on September 16, 1948. Note the ex-BR&P wooden caboose ahead of the 2-10-2.

(Bruce D. Fales, Jay Williams collection)

(above) T-3 #5581 is seen in Pennsylvania, on March 20, 1953, heading train #22 around an S-curve. After 1956, the impressive Mountain would become #723.

(William P. Price photo)

(above left) Pacific #5043 flies through Manila, Pennsylvania, climbing Sand Patch grade, on October 11, 1949, with train #21.

(William P. Price photo)

(below left) Making an almost royal appearance, #2, the *Lord Baltimore*, speeds by us at Ivy Yard, in Washington, on February 9, 1936, pulling the Royal Blue, and trailing a white plume of smoke in the cold air. It is 4:20 p.m., and the sun is already starting to set on the beautiful Hudson-type locomotive.

(Bruce D. Fales photo, Jay Williams collection)

(above) P-7 #5317 flies through Washington Grove, Maryland, on March 29, 1953. The sharp-looking Pacific, later #115 after the 1956 renumberings, is heading up express train #734.
(Bruce D. Fales photo, Jay Williams collection)

BIBLIOGRAPHY

B&O Railroad Company, The. *Renumbering and Reclassification of Locomotives and Diesel Rail Motor Cars.* Baltimore: B&O Railroad Co., 1956. (B&O Railroad Historical Society reproduction).

Barr, Howard N. and William A. Barringer. *Q: The Definitive History of The B&O Railroad Company's Q-Class Mikado Locomotives.* Baltimore: Barnard, Roberts and Co., 1978.

Dicken, Bruce K. and James M. Semon. *B&O Trackside With Willis A. McCaleb.* Scotch Plains, N.J.: Morning Sun Books, 1998.

Edson, William D. *Steam Locomotives of the B&O: An All-Time Roster.* Potomac, Maryland: William D. Edson, 1992.

Harwood, Herbert H., Jr. *Impossible Challenge.* Baltimore: Barnard, Roberts and Co., 1979.

Mainey, David T. *B&O Steam In Color.* Scotch Plains, N.J.: Morning Sun Books, 2001.

Roberts, Charles S. *Sand Patch.* Baltimore: Barnard, Roberts and Co., 1993.

———. *West End.* Baltimore: Barnard, Roberts and Co., 1991.

Sagle, Lawrence W. and Alvin F. Staufer. *B&O Power.* Medina, Ohio: Alvin Staufer, 1964.

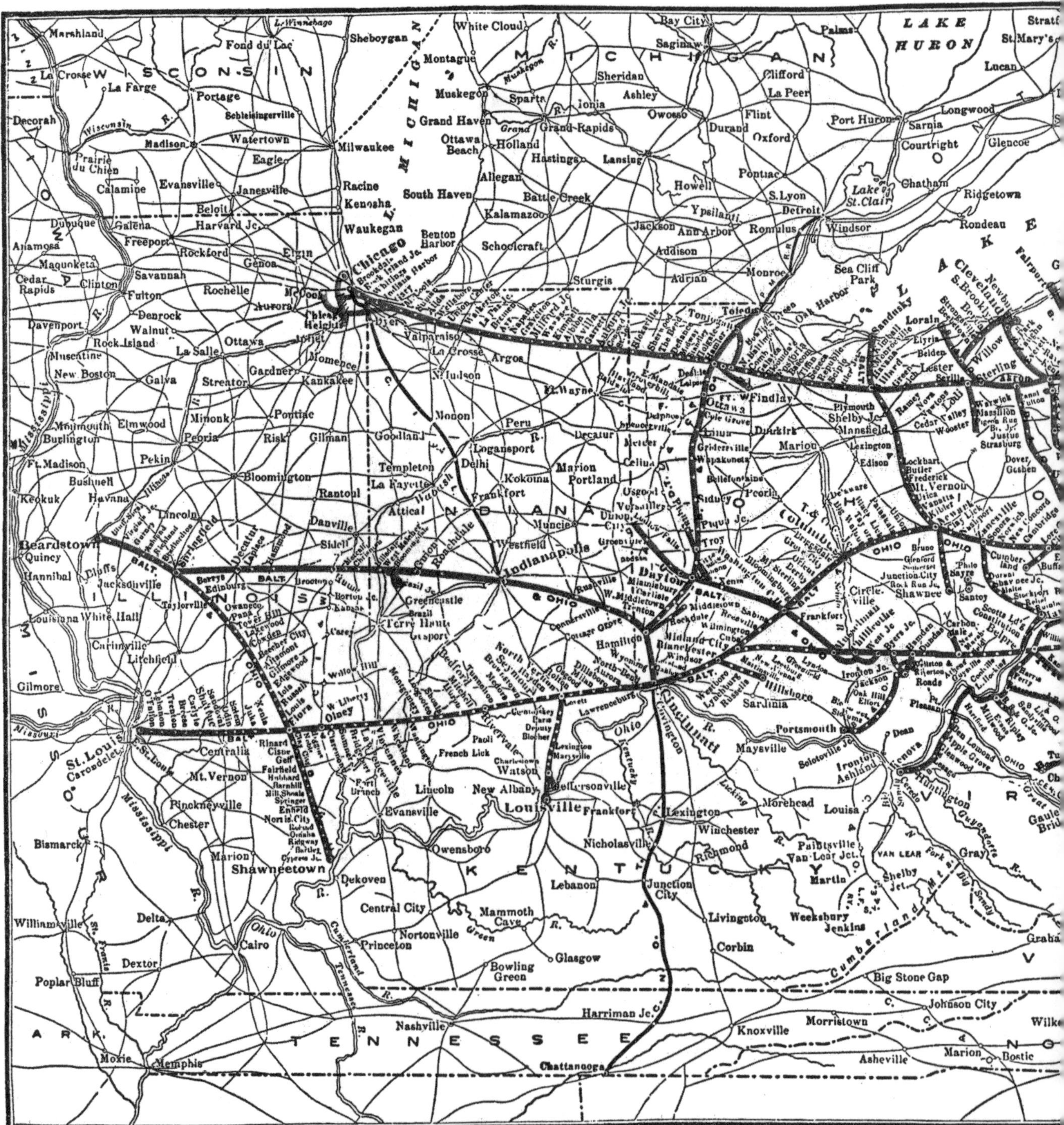

WISCONSIN
MICHIGAN
L. MICHIGAN
LAKE HURON
INDIANA
ILLINOIS
OHIO
KENTUCKY
TENNESSEE
IOWA
MISSOURI
ARK.
LAKE ERIE
Marshland
Fond du Lac
L. Winnebago
Sheboygan
White Cloud
Bay City
Saginaw
Palms
St. Mary's
La Crosse
La Farge
Portage
Montague
Muskegon
Sheridan
Ashley
Clifford
La Peer
Lucan
Decorah
Schleisingerville
Watertown
Milwaukee
Grand Haven
Grand Rapids
Sparta
Ionia
Owosso
Durand
Flint
Oxford
Port Huron
Sarnia
Longwood
Courtright
Glencoe
Madison
Eagle
Ottawa Beach
Holland
Hastings
Lansing
Prairie du Chien
Calamine
Evansville
Janesville
Racine
Kenosha
Waukegan
Allegan
South Haven
Battle Creek
Kalamazoo
Howell
Pontiac
S. Lyon
Ypsilanti
Detroit
Windsor
Lake St. Clair
Chatham
Ridgetown
Rondeau
Beloit
Harvard Jc.
Dubuque
Galena
Freeport
Rockford
Elgin
Genoa
Benton Harbor
Schoolcraft
Jackson
Ann Arbor
Romulus
Addison
Adrian
Monroe
Sea Cliff Park
Anamosa
Maquoketa
Cedar Rapids
Clinton
Savannah
Fulton
Rochelle
Chicago
Aurora
Chicago Heights
Sturgis
Toledo
Oak Harbor
Sandusky
Cleveland
Lorain
Elyria
Davenport
Denrock
Walnut
Rock Island
Muscatine
New Boston
La Salle
Ottawa
Valparaiso
La Crosse
Argos
Galva
Streator
Gardner
Momence
Kankakee
N. Judson
Ft. Wayne
Findlay
Ottawa
Akron
Sterling
Monmouth
Elmwood
Burlington
Minonk
Pontiac
Monon
Peru
Decatur
Delphos
Dunkirk
Plymouth
Shelby Jc.
Mansfield
Ft. Madison
Peoria
Pekin
Risk
Gilman
Goodland
Logansport
Celina
Marion
Lexington
Edison
Keokuk
Bushnell
Havana
Bloomington
Templeton
La Fayette
Delhi
Kokomo
Frankfort
Marion
Portland
Wapakoneta
Sidney
Peoria
Mt. Vernon
Lincoln
Rantoul
Attica
Muncie
Piqua
Troy
Columbus
Beardstown
Quincy
Springfield
Decatur
Danville
Sidell
Westfield
Indianapolis
Dayton
Xenia
Hannibal
Jacksonville
Edinburg
Greencastle
Brazil
Terre Haute
Rushville
Connersville
Hamilton
Trenton
Middletown
Frankfort
Circleville
Shawnee
Louisiana
White Hall
Taylorville
Carlinville
Litchfield
Hamilton
Lawrenceburg
Cincinnati
Covington
Sardinia
Hillsboro
Portsmouth
Ironton
Gilmore
Olney
St. Louis
Carondelet
Centralia
Mt. Vernon
Paoli
French Lick
Watson
Maysville
Ashland
Huntington
Pinckneyville
Chester
Lincoln
Evansville
New Albany
Jeffersonville
Louisville
Frankfort
Lexington
Morehead
Louisa
Winchester
Bismarck
Marion
Shawneetown
Owensboro
Nicholasville
Richmond
Paintsville
Van Lear Jct.
Martin
Gray
Dekoven
Lebanon
Junction City
Central City
Mammoth Cave
Williamsville
Delta
Cairo
Princeton
Nortonville
Livingston
Weeksbury
Jenkins
Dexter
Glasgow
Corbin
Poplar Bluff
Bowling Green
Big Stone Gap
Cumberland Mts.
Johnson City
Harriman Jc.
Nashville
Knoxville
Morristown
Moxie
Memphis
Chattanooga
Asheville
Marion
Bostic